Lord, What Do You Want Me To Know Today?

Sandra Bonk

Lord, What Do You Want Me To Know Today?

Copyright © 2019 Sandra Bonk

Scripture taken from the Holy Bible, New International Version®. NIV®. Copyright © 1973, 1978, 1984 by International Bible Society. Used by permission of Zondervan. All rights reserved.

ISBN-13: 978-1-08854-152-4

DEDICATED TO OUR CREATOR AND LORD, AND TO those family members and many friends He placed in my life who supported me and encouraged me to keep moving forward on this project in obedience to His calling.

Introduction

Lord, What Do You Want Me To Know Today?

I think we've all experienced that "Aha!" moment when something we've learned in the past becomes suddenly new and exciting to us again. That is what I have been blessed with daily as I seek God through reading His Holy Word, journaling my prayers, and spending quiet time in His Presence. I believe the entries in this book are reminders to me from God. He has reminded me of truths, principles, and scriptures I have learned from reading His Holy Word, from hearing sermons, and from reading books written by other Christians.

Earlier in my life, God gave me the gift of writing piano music and songs, which I believe gave me a way to worship Him more deeply. More recently, I believe God has also given me the gift of "hearing" what He impresses upon my heart during my quiet times with Him so that I might know Him more personally.

I am sharing my journal entries with the hope that readers will likewise be encouraged in their walk with God.

~ Sandra Bonk

Me: "Lord, what do You want me to know today?"

God: "Come to Me with every detail of your life. Tell Me your ideas and plans—how you want to see your dreams fulfilled. I will take you under My wing and shelter you as I show you what will work and what will not.

"You will be amazed at the way your dreams can be achieved with greater purpose when you let Me be involved in the writing of your story. I have chapters to insert that you haven't considered as a possibility in the big picture of your life."

Ps. 25:4 (NIV) ~ "Show me your ways, O Lord, teach me your paths."

Me: "Lord, what do You want me to know today?"

God: "Watch for My signals to you when you falter in your faith walk. I will give you signs that cannot be mistaken for mere coincidence or happenstance. I will direct your ways in unmistakable patterns that you will learn to recognize if you keep your spiritual eyes open and trained on Me.

"Come to Me with every burden, and lay them at My feet —multiple times, if necessary. I am making a new design, a work of art, from the pieces of your life that you are surrendering to My care bit by bit. You will be astounded to one day see the finished masterpiece that has been formed from all that you and I have accomplished together throughout your life on earth. I am not finished with you yet!"

Ps. 16:8 (NIV) ~ "I have set the Lord always before me. Because He is at my right hand, I will not be shaken."

Me: "Lord, what do You want me to know today?"

God: "When you wait on Me to direct your paths, you can be sure you will not falter. I will give you the necessary means to reach your goals. Take what I give you and run with it—do not stop to worry about what anyone else thinks, or what it looks like to others."

Prov. 4:11-12 (NIV) ~ "I guide you in the way of wisdom and lead you along straight paths. When you walk, your steps will not be hampered; when you run, you will not stumble."

Me: "Lord, what do You want me to know today?"

God: "When you hear My voice and listen to Me with a willing spirit, I will give you everything your heart needs to know to be able to decipher My will for your life. Let Me into your deepest, secret places. Let Me shine My light there to expose whatever needs to be brought under examination and dealt with according to My purpose for you. The result will be a stunning transformation, a work of My hand that will bring you up out of the ashes and into a position of being able to minister to others in likewise situations.

"I have a higher calling for you than you can imagine, a purpose beyond following your own whims. Search your heart and come to Me with everything. Lay it all out for Me to see, given freely by your own hands into My safe-keeping."

1 Pet. 2:9 (NIV) ~ "But you are a chosen people, a royal priesthood, a holy nation, a people belonging to God, that you may declare the praises of him who called you out of darkness into his wonderful light."

Me: "Lord, what do You want me to know today?"

God: "You matter to Me more than you know. I will spend eternity showing you how important you are to Me.

"Let Me give you My best for you; I have it all worked out already. Just show up each day and hold out your hands. I will pour out My good measure of provision for you to embrace and share with others. You will have enough, always."

Nahum 1:7 (NIV) ~ "The Lord is good, a refuge in times of trouble. He cares for those who trust in him,"

Me: "Lord, what do You want me to know today?"

God: "Surely, you will remember all I have taught you about Myself over the years, about how I am preparing a place for You in My heavenly Kingdom. With all authority in heaven and on earth, I have placed My Spirit within you to dwell there and to guide you, for My righteousness' sake. Have no fear for your future—I am taking you on a journey I created just for you. You will be entrusted with much responsibility. Do not seek to know answers I'm not ready to reveal to you yet.

"Trust Me to perfect the flaws along your path in a way that points to My Divine intervention in an unmistakable manner. Remain steadfast in Me, and let Me work out the delicate details you fuss about. You will see how I've arranged everything to fall into place at the right time. In all you do, let My praise be on your lips, that others may know the reason for your joy."

Ps. 33:21 (NIV) ~ "In him our hearts rejoice, for we trust in his holy name."

Me: "Lord, what do You want me to know today?"

God: "Arise each morning with words of praise on your lips, for the breath in your lungs is a gift from Me. I desire your acknowledgment of My love for you. When you honor Me this way, you bring glory to My Holy Name. A thankful heart, despite your circumstances, is refreshing evidence of your unwavering faith in Me."

Ps. 13:5-6 (NIV) ~ "But I trust in your unfailing love; my heart rejoices in your salvation. I will sing the Lord's praise, for he has been good to me."

Me: "Lord, what do You want me to know today?"

God: "When you place your concerns at My feet, I will replace them with contentment that comes from being sure of Whose you are. You are My child, and I will give you grace that is sufficient for every need you face.

"I am cultivating a spirit of self-confidence and greater purpose within you that will require your wholehearted faith in My guidance for your life. Stop at nothing when you sense My nudge to act upon those situations I will reveal to you which require an immediate response. Let Me handle the outcome of your obedience."

Phil. 4:12-13 (NIV) ~ "I know what it is to be in need, and I know what it is to have plenty. I have learned the secret of being content in any and every situation, whether well fed or hungry, whether living in plenty or in want. I can do all this through him who gives me strength."

Me: "Lord, what do You want me to know today?"

God: "You are struggling with obeying Me in the ways you know are necessary for the furthering of My gospel in the lives of those you touch. Keep looking to Me for your strength when you are weak.

"Keep obeying My nudges to reach out to others in unconditional love and acceptance. I am working out something amazing in your life. You will be astonished at what I can and will accomplish through you."

Luke 11:28 (NIV) ~ "He replied, 'Blessed rather are those who hear the word of God and obey it.'"

Me: "Lord, what do You want me to know today?"

God: "I will teach you My ways if you truly desire to learn from Me. Keep loving all who cross your path, and I will keep giving you the grace to accomplish My will as you seek to honor Me.

"Don't give up on your dreams—they are the culmination of all I desire to give you, in a nutshell. There will be weeping and rejoicing in the coming days. Never forget that I am holding you in the storm."

Ps. 119:68 (NIV) ~ "You are good, and what you do is good; teach me your decrees."

Me: "Lord, what do You want me to know today?"

God: "Say with all your heart, and mean it completely, 'I trust You, O, my God, to carry out the will of Your heart in my life.' This is the way to receive all I give you, with thanksgiving."

Ps. 40:4 (NIV) ~ "Blessed is the one who trusts in the Lord, who does not look to the proud, to those who turn aside to false gods."

Me: "Lord, what do You want me to know today?"

God: "With all that I've given you, there will be those who seek to pull you down, to see you come to ruin. Make obedience to Me a top priority, and nothing I've given you will go to waste.

"There is a right time for everything; when I show you a path to take, follow it unswervingly, and it will lead you to the destination I have for you. Your purpose on this earth will be carried out in a way that glorifies Me and delights you. There is nothing you could imagine that I can't give you at the right time. Trust Me with all your heart and see if I make your dreams come true."

Num. 11:23 (NIV) ~ "The Lord answered Moses, 'Is the Lord's arm too short? You will now see whether or not what I say will come true for you.'"

Me: "Lord, what do You want me to know today?"

God: "How I resonate with love for you; how My heart has been poured out into your life through so many people I've placed in your presence; how I will take you to heights that will take your breath away if you will but trust in Me to work out every detail.

"I am for you and not against you. Believe the best is yet to come."

1 John 4:15-16 (NIV) ~ "If anyone acknowledges that Jesus is the Son of God, God lives in them and they in God. And so we know and rely on the love God has for us. God is love. Whoever lives in love lives in God, and God in them."

Me: "Lord, what do You want me to know today?"

God: "I am the same yesterday, today, and always. Believe that I have My hand upon you and everyone you care for.

"Be diligent in showing My love to all whom you come in contact with. Be sure to concentrate on the needs of others, putting them ahead of your wants and desires. Then, you will see and feel My joy being revealed in your life; you will shine like the morning sun."

1 John 4:19 (NIV) ~ "We love because he first loved us."

Me: "Lord, what do You want me to know today?"

God: "Lay your burdens at My feet, and wait for My directions to you regarding further action. I will use these offerings to embolden you to take the next step toward completing My purpose in your life. When you empty your hands of your cherished treasures and relinquish these to Me, I will make known to you the vast resources of My Kingdom that are yours to delight in.

"You will know no end to the riches of My love for you as you bask in My light continually, and your faith will be seen by all who gaze upon your life—a life of communion with Me."

Rom. 11:33 (NIV) ~ "Oh, the depth of the riches of the wisdom and knowledge of God! How unsearchable his judgments, and his paths beyond tracing out!"

Me: "Lord, what do You want me to know today?"

God: "When you find that I've been right beside you at work in every situation, ironing out every detail, you will not cease to rejoice in My Divine intervention. Looking back one day, you will see how I loved you too much to let you fall at the enemy's bidding. He seeks to destroy all traces of your allegiance to Me.

"Pour yourself into My work and devote your heart to My safekeeping. I will fend off the weapons of destruction being aimed at you. I will be your strength in time of need. Call on My Name, and I will hear you and rescue you every time. You are My beloved child, and I will continue to show you how precious you are to me. Believe I've got this!"

Eph. 3:16 (NIV) ~ "I pray that out of his glorious riches he may strengthen you with power through his Spirit in your inner being,"

Me: "Lord, what do You want me to know today?"

God: "I will reveal to you what I want you to know at the appropriate times. Keep searching for My truth every chance you get, and I will teach you about your character strengths and weaknesses.

"Give Me your burdens on a regular basis, that I may carry them for you, and look to Me for guidance in the areas where you can't see clearly right now. I am already going ahead of you, preparing the way for you to follow Me without hesitation."

Prov. 2:3-5 (NIV) ~ "indeed, if you call out for insight and cry aloud for understanding, and if you look for it as for silver and search for it as for hidden treasure, then you will understand the fear of the Lord and find the knowledge of God."

Me: "Lord, what do You want me to know today?"

God: "When it seems that circumstances are getting you down, remember I am at work in your life. Trust Me as I rearrange events in your day or your week, for this is for someone's good, though it may feel like a huge inconvenience to you.

"Will you let Me share with you the plans I have for you if they don't match up to your expectations? Do you trust Me enough to believe I have an awesome future in store for you? Let's move forward together!"

Ps. 119:35 (NIV) ~ "Direct me in the path of your commands, for there I find delight."

Me: "Lord, what do You want me to know today?"

God: "Having a plan and a purpose for your life is a good idea, but be willing to bend when I tweak your plans here and there.

"Keep moving in the direction you sense Me leading you until you come to a standstill; then, I will redirect you. There will be no wasted efforts on your part because I will teach you something through every effort you make toward fulfilling your purpose."

Hos. 14:9 (NIV) ~ "Who is wise? Let them realize these things. Who is discerning? Let them understand. The ways of the Lord are right; the righteous walk in them, but the rebellious stumble in them."

Me: "Lord, what do You want me to know today?"

God: "Some things will be difficult for you to understand in the coming days, but you will have My strength and insight when you need them. Apply what I've taught you to each situation you face, and there will be no cause for concern about the future.

"When the enemy comes lurking, stand your ground on My Word, repeating My truths over and over as needed until you truly believe them, and he will flee every time."

1 Pet. 5:8-9 (NIV) ~ "Be alert and of sober mind. Your enemy the devil prowls around like a roaring lion looking for someone to devour. Resist him, standing firm in the faith, because you know that the family of believers throughout the world is undergoing the same kind of sufferings."

Me: "Lord, what do You want me to know today?"

God: "Submit your desires to Me, and I will show you how I can use those desires to fulfill My purpose in your life. There will be nothing I can't accomplish through your willingness to lean on Me and be used by Me, even as you wait for your hopes and dreams to materialize.

"I will weave your life into a beautiful pattern of blessing to others, who will in turn rejoice and bless My Name because of your giving to the Lord even in your emptiness."

Ps. 20:4 (NIV) ~ "May he give you the desire of your heart and make all your plans succeed."

Me: "Lord, what do You want me to know today?"

God: "I am setting before you a higher standard to follow, regarding My decrees for your life. You have been called by Me to be a messenger of light. Do not let your light waver in the midst of the darkness that surrounds it.

"Be strong and courageous in the face of opposition from the enemy. He has no power over you—stand on My Word and proclaim it with victory! You are Mine! I am producing in you a tenacity that will drive you to not only endure your hardships but to strive harder and thrive in the midst of adversity as you carry out My plans for your ministry and mission in life. Trust Me with every gem you treasure in your heart. Your most valued, fantastical dreams are safe with Me."

James 1:12 (NIV) ~ "Blessed is the one who perseveres under trial because, having stood the test, that person will receive the crown of life that the Lord has promised to those who love him."

Me: "Lord, what do You want me to know today?"

God: "When you feel abandoned by those you depend on, realize that this is a time of stretching and strengthening for your heart and soul. I am allowing these experiences so you will come to understand how much you need to rely on Me, solely.

"No human being can fulfill your greatest need, which is to be loved and cherished completely and unconditionally, one hundred percent of the time. Only I can do that, and I will do that. I am always here for you."

Ps. 36:7 (NIV) ~ "How priceless is your unfailing love, O God! People take refuge in the shadow of your wings."

Me: "Lord, what do You want me to know today?"

God: "My Child, when you come to Me in prayer, and willingness to listen to Me, I am honored by your sacrifice of time spent with Me in communion. I will show you what this means to Me by the way I reinforce the things you are learning, in unexpected ways, and at any given time."

Job 36:22 (NIV) ~ "God is exalted in his power. Who is a teacher like him?"

Me: "Lord, what do You want me to know today?"

God: "When I show you a truth from My Word, I will help you understand what it means, so you can practice applying it to your life. Remember that everything you learn from reading My Word is going to enable you to become more Christ-like, and your light will shine brighter for those in darkness to see. Then, you will become more usable by Me for the purpose of sharing My goodness and love with a hurting world.

"I have big plans for you. Stand firm when the waves of doubt and fear crash against you; I have a hold on you—I will guide you through the storms ahead. Trust in Me completely, and rejoice over all I am going to do in your life, for it will be good and praiseworthy."

2 Cor. 4:6 (NIV) ~ "For God, who said, 'Let light shine out of darkness,' made his light shine in our hearts to give us the light of the knowledge of God's glory displayed in the face of Christ."

Me: "Lord, what do You want me to know today?"

God: "Just when you think you have everything figured out, you will see that I have an even greater plan for your life.

"Go ahead and make your plans. Then, be ready for what I will do to transform your ideas into workable solutions that will enable you to complete the purpose I've given you to carry out. You will see how My hand has guided you all along the way, and you will know the satisfaction that stems from a heart of willingness and obedience to My will."

Ps. 89:15-16 (NIV) ~ "Blessed are those who have learned to acclaim you, who walk in the light of your presence, Lord. They rejoice in your name all day long; they celebrate your righteousness."

Me: "Lord, what do You want me to know today?"

God: "Tell Me what you want, and why, and I will tell you what I expect of you in order to lead you in that direction. Trust Me when you don't see how things will work out. I see the whole picture.

"I am taking you on a journey of discovery—the discovery of who I made you to be, and I will show you what your heart longs for as you commune with Me daily. Don't give up on Me or yourself, for all that lies ahead will astound you, and I will place My shield of protection around you to ward off the enemy's attacks, which will surely come."

Ps. 33:20 (NIV) ~ "We wait in hope for the Lord; he is our help and our shield."

Me: "Lord, what do You want me to know today?"

God: "While it seems to you like I am not hearing your heart's desires, what is really happening as you wait is this: I am sifting the valuable treasures of your heart through My fingers and letting the things fall away that blind you from seeing My truth and your worth.

"When your heart is free of destructive thought patterns, you will be more open to My leading, and I will reveal more of Myself to you as you seek to obey Me fully in all you do. Then, you will know the fullness of joy, and you will be ready to move forward and embrace all that I've prepared for you. Your delight will be My delight, and you will not walk alone on this journey."

Ps. 36:9 (NIV) ~ "For with you is the fountain of life; in your light we see light."

Me: "Lord, what do You want me to know today?"

God: "How much I love you! When you do acts of love to others, you do them to Me. I will show you how to love others as I love them; all you need to do is obey My nudging when it comes. Show them that love has no borders, no boundaries, and that it covers a multitude of sins.

"You will be blessed through the giving and pouring-out process, and you will be filled up in such a way that will allow you to keep pouring out life-giving love into the lives of those who are so thirsty for it. Do not hold back and keep for yourself that which is meant to be broken and shared and poured out."

Rom. 13:8 (NIV) ~ "Let no debt remain outstanding, except the continuing debt to love one another, for whoever loves others has fulfilled the law."

Me: "Lord, what do You want me to know today?"

God: "I am changing the way you think about Me as you spend more time with Me, and in My Word. You are being transformed, with My light shining through more of your broken pieces and My love restoring you to be wholly usable for My kingdom work in your life.

"Keep drawing from the resources I provide for you every time you feel yourself falling, failing, crumbling under pressure, and you will know the freedom found when you let Me bear your burdens. I am here for you. I know everything you struggle with, and nothing you go through will destroy you because there is unlimited power in My Name, and that power is yours to call upon whenever you need it. I love you with an everlasting love."

Ps. 56:13 (NIV) ~ "For you have delivered me from death and my feet from stumbling, that I may walk before God in the light of life."

Me: "Lord, what do You want me to know today?"

God: "What you have experienced in your life has made you more compassionate toward others. Use what you have learned to cultivate positive, loving relationships with those people I connect you with. Be the one who breaks the pattern of condemnation and rivalry. Be willing to stand out as 'different' in the world's eyes."

Zech. 7:9-10 (NIV) ~ "This is what the Lord Almighty said: 'Administer true justice; show mercy and compassion to one another. Do not oppress the widow or the fatherless, the foreigner or the poor. Do not plot evil against each other.'"

Me: "Lord, what do You want me to know today?"

God: "What seems like hardship or inconvenience to you will actually turn out to be a blessing if you embrace it with thankfulness to Me. When you treat others as you'd like to be treated, you will reap the blessing of My givenness, broken and poured out for you.

"You will be restored and refilled as you seek to uplift others, rather than tear them down. I am with you always, and My Spirit will nudge you when I want you to act on behalf of the needy. Do not ignore the nudging of the Spirit."

Matt. 7:12 (NIV) ~ "So in everything, do to others what you would have them do to you, for this sums up the Law and the Prophets."

Me: "Lord, what do You want me to know today?"

God: "Reserve quality time in your day to be spent with Me, alone. Be prepared to spend time in prayer on behalf of others, whomever I lay on your heart, plus those you know who have needs. Expect to see answers to your prayers—they will come when I know the time is right. Be diligent. Never stop praying and believing. Your faithful prayers can move mountains."

Ps. 86:7 (NIV) ~ "When I am in distress, I call to you, because you answer me."

Me: "Lord, what do You want me to know today?"

God: "When you see how I am weaving your days and life experiences together to create a vision of My will for your life, you will find it easier to move forward and walk in the direction I am leading you. I will show you through circumstances how much I value your complete trust in Me. I will bless your obedience to Me, which will encourage others to do the same when I prick their hearts, also."

Ps. 5:12 (NIV) ~ "Surely, Lord, you bless the righteous; you surround them with your favor as with a shield."

Me: "Lord, what do You want me to know today?"

God: "Let Me take you to a higher place of communion with Me. There, I will show you why obedience to Me is so important, and the effects it will have on your relationships with your family and friends. Do not think for a moment that I intend to punish you every time you fall, but know that I am right here beside you to pick you up and brush you off so you can continue the journey with Me.

"I have great insight into your unique situation, and I am unraveling the tangled areas of your life so that you may be free to become the beautiful representation of My deepest longing for you (that which I've created in you)— a child after My own heart, using the gifts and talents I've given you, and reaping great joy from doing so."

Rom. 2:13 (NIV) ~ "For it is not those who hear the law who are righteous in God's sight, but it is those who obey the law who will be declared righteous."

Me: "Lord, what do You want me to know today?"

God: "When the walls are closing in, and the pressures in your life are mounting, do not hesitate to cry out to Me. I will hear your cries and will answer you. I will rescue you from the snares of the enemy. You only need to keep your eyes fixed on Me, and I will be your Vision."

Prov. 14:27 (NIV) ~ "The fear of the Lord is a fountain of life, turning a person from the snares of death."

Me: "Lord, what do You want me to know today?"

God: "I have so much to share with you—things you would never find out on your own. I can teach you what no man has the ability to teach, and I can show you the depths of My love for you in ways you cannot fathom. Reach out to Me, and I will carry you in the direction of the path I want you to follow next.

"Do you trust Me with all your heart? Have I ever let you down? I am doing something amazing in your life—you just can't see it yet."

Is. 28:26 (NIV) ~ "His God instructs him and teaches him the right way."

Me: "Lord, what do You want me to know today?"

God: "Let go of those thoughts that are weighing you down today—thoughts that you have let people down; thoughts that you've missed a lot of great opportunities to love people in your life. Today is a new day, a new chance to love the people I've put in your life—do so with joy and enthusiasm. Bless others, whenever and however I provide opportunities, and you yourself will be greatly blessed also."

Prov. 15:23 (NIV) ~ "A person finds joy in giving an apt reply—and how good is a timely word!"

Me: "Lord, what do You want me to know today?"

God: "You are never alone. I am always here with you, and I will always give you the abilities you need, to do the purpose at hand, for any given moment."

Ps. 68:35 (NIV) ~ "You, God, are awesome in your sanctuary; the God of Israel gives power and strength to his people. Praise be to God!"

Me: "Lord, what do You want me to know today?"

God: "Plans for your future are being secured already by My own hand. Trust Me to continue filling in the blanks where your dreams and desires are concerned. Remove all doubt from your heart and forge forward with all certainty and faith in your Father's discernment. I will not let you down. You have been created with a greater purpose than you can imagine."

Is. 26:4 (NIV) ~ "Trust in the Lord forever, for the Lord, the Lord himself, is the Rock eternal."

Me: "Lord, what do You want me to know today?"

God: "Stay close to Me through reading My Word and through prayer. I have put people in your life to encourage you in your walk with Me; reach out to them—don't wait for them to ask how you're doing in this area."

Ps. 73:28 (NIV) ~ "But as for me, it is good to be near God. I have made the Sovereign Lord my refuge; I will tell of all your deeds."

Me: "Lord, what do You want me to know today?"

God: "Listen to Me when I say this: You have been given specific tasks to complete in your lifetime. Whether they get done or not depends on your willingness to set aside the less important things and say 'no' to yourself whenever necessary."

Is. 1:19 (NIV) ~ "If you are willing and obedient, you will eat the good things of the land;"

Me: "Lord, what do You want me to know today?"

God: "Use every opportunity I give you to fulfill My calling in your life. Focus on the eternal rather than the temporal, and you will be fruitful for My Kingdom."

2 Cor. 4:18 (NIV) ~ "So we fix our eyes not on what is seen, but on what is unseen, since what is seen is temporary, but what is unseen is eternal."

Me: "Lord, what do You want me to know today?"

God: "Submit your desires into My safekeeping and leave the outcome to Me. When the time is right, you shall be given the tools you need to complete the work I've assigned you. Until then, keep working on what I've already given you to do, and take joy in knowing that the best is yet to come."

2 Cor. 4:17 (NIV) ~ "For our light and momentary troubles are achieving for us an eternal glory that far outweighs them all."

Me: "Lord, what do You want me to know today?"

God: "Stop trying to weigh the consequences of your own actions versus Mine, in your life. You know My ways are best. You know I have nothing but good in store for you as you obey Me willingly. Let Me show you My undying love for you in the ways I provide for you everything you need. Let Me be your shelter in every storm—no harm shall befall you."

Ps. 103:17 (NIV) ~ "But from everlasting to everlasting the Lord's love is with those who fear him, and his righteousness with their children's children—"

Me: "Lord, what do You want me to know today?"

God: "See what I have done in your life so far—take note of the many ways I've brought you through fire and redeemed your life when you felt all seemed hopeless. I have been beside you every step of the way, and I will continue to be with you as you walk forward from this day on."

Lam. 3:57-58 (NIV) ~ "You came near when I called you, and you said, 'Do not fear.' You, Lord, took up my case; you redeemed my life."

February 16

Me: "Lord, what do You want me to know today?"

God: "I will stand with you when the enemy attacks. He shall not cut you down when I am holding you up. I will be your strength; hold onto Me and be encouraged. Together we have so many joys to discover and tasks to complete.

"Every day is a new chance for Me to show you how much I love you, and I will do just that. Keep your eyes on Me and follow My leading throughout your day."

Ps. 118:14 (NIV) ~ "The Lord is my strength and my defense; he has become my salvation."

Me: "Lord, what do You want me to know today?"

God: "When I show you glimpses of My plans for your life, do not doubt that I will incorporate your dreams into those plans. Be steadfast in your work, and do not dwell on what isn't happening right now. Rejoice that I have chosen you to carry out something much bigger than yourself in this lifetime I've given you. I know what it will take, and who you will need to help you complete this work. I've already begun to prepare your heart for the emotional ride that lies ahead. Stay forward-focused, and believe that I have everything under control at all times."

Ps. 9:2 (NIV) ~ "I will be glad and rejoice in you; I will sing the praises of your name, O Most High."

Me: "Lord, what do You want me to know today?"

God: "I have given you much to think about through My Word, and much work to do for My kingdom purpose. When you set your heart on serving Me completely, I will guide your way in every task you put your hands to. You will not need to question My direction for your life, because I will reveal to you that which you need to know, exactly when you need it."

Luke 4:8 (NIV) ~ "Jesus answered, "It is written: 'Worship the Lord your God and serve him only.'""

Me: "Lord, what do You want me to know today?"

God: "I am building your future, one block at a time. Each block needs to be sturdy enough to support other blocks that will be placed atop them as time passes. Allow Me to strengthen you in the areas you need, so you will be ready for what I am preparing for you in the days ahead."

2 Thess. 3:3 (NIV) ~ "But the Lord is faithful, and he will strengthen you and protect you from the evil one."

Me: "Lord, what do You want me to know today?"

God: "Be the light to those who are suffering. You will know who you need to encourage; act upon it, and I will go before you to prepare the way. Do not be afraid of the response you will get. Share My love unashamedly. You will get better at it the more you do it."

1 Thess. 5:5 (NIV) ~ "You are all children of the light and children of the day. We do not belong to the night or to the darkness."

Me: "Lord, what do You want me to know today?"

God: "When you see Me at work in your life, don't ask Me why I'm allowing certain circumstances to occur. Just trust Me with the outcomes, and I will keep your heart and mind in perfect peace as you do so. Let Me rearrange your plans in a way that I know will be best for you. Then you will see the fulfillment of your greatest dreams at just the right time!"

Ps. 138:8 (NIV) ~ "The Lord will vindicate me; your love, Lord, endures forever—do not abandon the works of your hands."

Me: "Lord, what do You want me to know today?"

God: "When it seems like there is no definite plan for your future, that is when I am able to step in and orchestrate something beautiful without your interference. When you allow Me to create a script for your life that no one but you can live out, then you will know My peace and the fulfillment that comes from doing what you were created to do. Your joy will be uncontainable."

Jer. 32:17 (NIV) ~ "Ah, Sovereign Lord, you have made the heavens and the earth by your great power and outstretched arm. Nothing is too hard for you."

Me: "Lord, what do You want me to know today?"

God: "Of all the ways a man could choose to live his life, the most fulfilling to his soul will be one of humble submission to My will for him. I have given you the freedom to pursue whatever your heart desires; however, you and I both know that some of your desires will lead you to a dead-end, spiritually. I have so much life to pour into you in your remaining days on earth.

"Let Me show you how amazing My love for you is in so many tangible ways as you walk closely with Me. I will help you pursue those things that will bring you the greatest joy, and you will glorify Me in doing so as you use the gifts and talents I've given you."

Ps. 149:4 (NIV) ~ "For the Lord takes delight in his people; he crowns the humble with victory."

Me: "Lord, what do You want me to know today?"

God: "Be ready to carry out My purposes for your life. Only then will you find true satisfaction in those things that seem meaningless to you at this time. I will show you how everything you put your hand to can be used to further My kingdom work in your areas of influence.

"You will find that I have given you much more ability to be encouraging to others, for My Name's sake, than you ever imagined. All it will take is a willing heart and a contrite spirit. I will accomplish much through your obedience to My every nudging when I send you someone in need of unconditional love and acceptance. Reach out to those who have no one else to come alongside them. Be a light in the darkness."

Is. 66:2 (NIV) ~ "These are the ones I look on with favor: those who are humble and contrite in spirit, and who tremble at my word."

Me: "Lord, what do You want me to know today?"

God: "When I make known to you those things I want you to accomplish for My kingdom purpose, I will also provide all you need, in order for you to complete the tasks I've set before you. Do not hesitate to move forward in faith when I urge you to do so. You will see My hand at work alongside you, and you will be encouraged even as you encourage others through your diligent acts of obedience to Me.

"Your life will have greater purpose when you serve others with a heart of thanksgiving, thinking not about what it will cost you in the end. I will always give you enough: enough time, enough patience, enough ability, enough wisdom, enough love to share with another who is in need. Trust Me to go before you to open doors when necessary. Your job is to just obey—keep moving. We've got this!"

Phil. 4:13 (NIV) ~ "I can do all this through him who gives me strength."

Me: "Lord, what do You want me to know today?"

God: "When you sense My Presence leading you into situations that feel awkward or uncomfortable to you, do not resist My nudging—keep moving forward. I will take you to new heights of understanding what it means to represent My love to the needy and hurting souls around you. There will be blessings that come from your obedience to Me, though you may not see them in your lifetime. Do not give up. Do not back down. Run the race with perseverance, even when you can't see the finish line.

"I am giving you every opportunity to fulfill your purpose on this earth. Don't ignore My prompting when it comes; you will know the joy of the Lord, and I will be delighted with your sacrifice for My Name's sake."

Heb. 12:1 (NIV) ~ "Therefore, since we are surrounded by such a great cloud of witnesses, let us throw off everything that hinders and the sin that so easily entangles. And let us run with perseverance the race marked out for us."

Me: "Lord, what do You want me to know today?"

God: "I am with you in every situation. I know how you feel at any given moment. Never doubt My love for you as you seek to know My will.

"There are things I allow you to go through that will strengthen your faith in Me. One day you will see and understand the reasons for what you've been through, and you will know I've always had your best interests in mind and your deepest concerns close to My heart. I am for you and not against you—always. Remember that!"

Matt. 28:20 (NIV) ~ "...And surely I am with you always, to the very end of the age."

Me: "Lord, what do You want me to know today?"

God: "I will lead you through any uncertain situations you find yourself in today. Trust Me to guide you in confidence as you place your hand in Mine. We will conquer this day together!"

Rom. 8:37 (NIV) ~ "No, in all these things we are more than conquerors through him who loved us."

Me: "Lord, what do You want me to know today?"

God: "Come to Me with every concern, large or small. Let Me share your burdens and help you carry the load you bear. I will always be here for you to lean on. You don't have to walk this path alone. Trust Me to lead you in the right direction.

"I will show you how to be satisfied with My provision for you, even as you take the next step forward toward that place where your dreams and My plans for you intersect in a beautiful display of faith and fulfillment."

Is. 41:10 (NIV) ~ "So do not fear, for I am with you; do not be dismayed, for I am your God. I will strengthen you and help you; I will uphold you with my righteous right hand."

Me: "Lord, what do You want me to know today?"

God: "When I give you My word about something I'm doing in your life, believe that I will finish what I started on your behalf; the results will always reflect My great love for you.

"Never doubt that what you are going through has a meaningful purpose which I am working out for your ultimate good. You will be given an understanding of what's happening when I feel you are ready to receive it. In the meantime, wait and be watchful for My guidance, which will lead you in the right direction as you continue to step forward in faith."

Phil. 1:6 (NIV) ~ "being confident of this, that he who began a good work in you will carry it on to completion until the day of Christ Jesus."

Me: "Lord, what do You want me to know today?"

God: "When you ask Me to work out a problem on your behalf, you will need to trust Me to do as I see fit regarding the issue. Do not try to grab back out of My hands that which you've given to Me in prayer.

"When things don't seem to be going in a direction you're comfortable with, just know that I have the ability to untwist or unravel circumstances before I smooth out any creases and tie the loose ends back together in a beautiful way. Let Me show you what I can do with your life when you offer it up to Me willingly."

Prov. 3:5-6 (NIV) ~ "Trust in the Lord with all your heart and lean not on your own understanding; in all your ways submit to him, and he will make your paths straight."

Me: "Lord, what do You want me to know today?"

God: "I have a purpose in mind for you. You were not put on this earth to seek your own pleasure—you were created to be a reflection of the heart of God.

"When you walk closely with Me, I will teach you about My great love for all people. You will see that you have been given an opportunity I designed only for you—a way to impact many hurting lives with the love of Christ Jesus, and in doing so, your cup of joy will be filled to overflowing. Do not miss this connection with Me! Nothing else you choose in life will even come close to the amazing plans I have for you!"

Phil. 2:13 (NIV) ~ "for it is God who works in you to will and to act in order to fulfill his good purpose."

Me: "Lord, what do You want me to know today?"

God: "When it seems like I am silent to your pleas for help, that is when I am working out a solution to your problem. Trust Me to make order out of the chaos in your life. As you trust Me, you will begin to feel more of My love for you, and I will teach you what I want you to know when the time is right.

"Always be ready to heed My call when I tell you to move into action. My purpose for you is greater than anything the world could distract you with. Be willing to be used by Me in ways that will reflect a heart of obedience."

Rom. 8:28 (NIV) ~ "And we know that in all things God works for the good of those who love him, who have been called according to his purpose."

Me: "Lord, what do You want me to know today?"

God: "I am here for you always. I will be your strength when you feel weak in your faith. I will uphold you with My righteous right hand when the enemy attacks you in ways that threaten your relationship with Me.

"Before you were formed in the womb, I laid out My design for your life. I also gave you a free will to choose for yourself whom you will serve. As you respond to My love for you, there will be no doubt in your mind that you were made for something so much larger than anything you've ever imagined or dreamed possible for yourself. Let Me show you how infinite My love for you is when you walk hand in hand with Me every day. There will be no end to the possibilities for accomplishing that which I created you for. Your joy will be limited only by your own choice to obey My calling or not."

Is. 41:10 (NIV) ~ "So do not fear, for I am with you; do not be dismayed, for I am your God. I will strengthen you and help you; I will uphold you with my righteous right hand."

Me: "Lord, what do You want me to know today?"

God: "Search your heart and see what is there that keeps you from responding to Me when I call your name. I have been waiting to teach you things that will show you how the pieces of your life, when put together, will form a beautiful picture that will reflect My gift of grace poured out upon you.

"Never doubt that every circumstance and every situation you've been through has been for a Divine purpose. When you willingly respond to My love, it is then that I will lead you toward the destination your heart longs for but doesn't know how to find. With My guidance, you will become like a refreshing rain on parched ground as you share with others what I've taught you."

Is. 58:11 (NIV) ~ "The Lord will guide you always; he will satisfy your needs in a sun-scorched land and will strengthen your frame. You will be like a well-watered garden, like a spring whose waters never fail."

Me: "Lord, what do You want me to know today?"

God: "Let Me carry your burdens today, so you may feel free to bask in My love and use your energy for those things which need to be accomplished before the day is done. By surrendering to Me those things that are weighing you down, you will receive greater satisfaction in knowing that your success is a result of your willingness to humble yourself in My sight. Humbleness is not a sign of weakness, but rather a sign of a teachable spirit."

Ps. 68:19 (NIV) ~ "Praise be to the Lord, to God our Savior, who daily bears our burdens."

Me: "Lord, what do You want me to know today?"

God: "There is always something I am working on in your life that needs refining. As you relinquish to Me the impurities filling the crevices of your heart, I will cleanse and renew you in such a way that you will be able to see with new eyes that which was always right in front of you —My greatest blessings created just for you."

Heb. 10:22 (NIV) ~ "let us draw near to God with a sincere heart and with the full assurance that faith brings, having our hearts sprinkled to cleanse us from a guilty conscience and having our bodies washed with pure water."

Me: "Lord, what do You want me to know today?"

God: "I see in you a heart of repentance that needs daily reminders of your great worth to Me. I am doing a work in your life that will reveal to you the many ways I love you. Do not be hesitant to come to Me when you feel overwhelmed by those things you have no control over. I will reassure you of My ability to walk you through any and every situation you face.

"There is nothing I can't use for good when it comes to your unique circumstances. As I piece together every moment of your journey to create a legacy of hope for future generations, I will also weave in evidence of My truth being exposed through your existence on this earth."

Rom. 12:12 (NIV) ~ "Be joyful in hope, patient in affliction, faithful in prayer."

Me: "Lord, what do You want me to know today?"

God: "I am standing in the gap for you, between what you think is best for you and what I know is best for you. Let Me have the chance to show you how deeply I care for you. Relinquish to Me everything you're trying to control on your own, and I will give you peace in return.

"Focus on those things which are eternal, and I will give you direction in your day-to-day activities, which will correlate with the growth you will experience spiritually. Trust Me in all things. I can work out any situation you struggle with."

Is. 30:21 (NIV) ~ "Whether you turn to the right or to the left, your ears will hear a voice behind you, saying, "This is the way; walk in it."

Me: "Lord, what do You want me to know today?"

God: "I will go before you and prepare the circumstances of your situation in a way that will bring My purpose for you into the right perspective, and will give you every reason to lean on Me in faith in future situations that concern you. Never doubt that I am working out a greater good from what you are going through."

Deut. 31:8 (NIV) ~ "The Lord himself goes before you and will be with you; he will never leave you nor forsake you. Do not be afraid; do not be discouraged."

Me: "Lord, what do You want me to know today?"

God: "I have seen in you a desire for a closer relation-ship with Me. When you put Me ahead of all else in your life, you will discover things about Me that you wouldn't know otherwise. I will show you what I'm doing in your life in a way that will bring you fulfillment and purpose, as you carry out every task I set before you with diligence and confidence."

Ps. 85:8 (NIV) ~ "I will listen to what God the Lord says; he promises peace to his people, his faithful servants— but let them not turn to folly."

Me: "Lord, what do You want me to know today?"

God: "I am preparing you for what I have planned for your future. When I lead you in one direction, do not try to figure out why—just follow Me. You will see how everything will work out, and how I have your best interests in My tender care at all times. You have nothing to fear. Trust Me in all things."

Eph. 2:10 (NIV) ~ "For we are God's handiwork, created in Christ Jesus to do good works, which God prepared in advance for us to do."

Me: "Lord, what do You want me to know today?"

God: "Whether you hear My voice or simply sense an urge to move forward in a manner that leads you to a place unfamiliar to you, it is then that you will know I am directing your path in a way that is more glorious than you can comprehend.

"Don't ignore Me when I want to show you something new. Instead, hold out your hands and receive all that I have for you. Together, you and I will share treasured moments that I'm saving just for you."

Matt. 25:23 (NIV) ~ "His master replied, 'Well done, good and faithful servant! You have been faithful with a few things; I will put you in charge of many things. Come and share your master's happiness!'"

Me: "Lord, what do You want me to know today?"

God: "I have seen your pain, your trials, your suffering, and I have been with you through it all. There is a good purpose for everything you've been through, and there will come a day when you will understand why I've allowed these things to take place, and you will see how My hand upheld you through it all.

"Trust that I am with you always, working something good out of all you struggle with."

1 Pet. 1:6-7 (NIV) ~ "In all this you greatly rejoice, though now for a little while you may have had to suffer grief in all kinds of trials. These have come so that the proven genuineness of your faith—of greater worth than gold, which perishes even though refined by fire—may result in praise, glory and honor when Jesus Christ is revealed."

Me: "Lord, what do You want me to know today?"

God: "Show Me how much the blessings in your life mean to you by the way you respond to Me each day. I have not given you less than you need to grow and thrive in your surroundings. Grasp hold of that which I've given you, and offer it all back to Me in sacrificial humbleness and thanksgiving, and I will multiply your blessings to overflowing."

Ps. 106:1 (NIV) ~ "Praise the Lord. Give thanks to the Lord, for he is good; his love endures forever."

Me: "Lord, what do You want me to know today?"

God: "Where there is suffering, there is also hope. Be ready to encourage others at all times. Be willing to be vulnerable and share the reason for your hope. Someone in your life needs to hear how I've transformed your despair into hope through the death and resurrection of My only Son, Jesus Christ, on the cross at Calvary.

"Your willingness to be a light in a dark world is evidence of your love for Me. I will give you the words to say when you need them. Just trust and obey."

1 Pet. 3:15 (NIV) ~ "But in your hearts revere Christ as Lord. Always be prepared to give an answer to everyone who asks you to give the reason for the hope that you have. But do this with gentleness and respect,"

Me: "Lord, what do You want me to know today?"

God: "When it seems to you that there is no clear direction for your future, that is when I am at work on your behalf, preparing your circumstances to be in alignment with My perfect will for your life. Before you step forward in any direction, ask Me to guide your steps, and your progress will be sure and steady."

Ps. 143:10 (NIV) ~ "Teach me to do your will, for you are my God; may your good Spirit lead me on level ground."

Me: "Lord, what do You want me to know today?"

God: "Wait on Me to instruct you when you can't see which path to take next. As you wait, there will be opportunities to explore, which will help you grow in your faith in My provision for you.

"There is no reason for you to grow stagnant while you wait on Me, for I will always provide new resources for you to learn from and contribute to, which will benefit more people than just yourself."

Col. 1:10 (NIV) ~ "so that you may live a life worthy of the Lord and please him in every way: bearing fruit in every good work, growing in the knowledge of God,"

Me: "Lord, what do You want me to know today?"

God: "The choices you make in every situation you face will ultimately shape the way you are perceived by others, and will either illuminate the way I am working in your life or dispel the hope you might have demonstrated through your dependence on Me.

"Always be mindful that your every action may have far-reaching consequences that will affect many others besides yourself."

Eph. 5:8 (NIV) ~ "For you were once darkness, but now you are light in the Lord. Live as children of light"

Me: "Lord, what do You want me to know today?"

God: "When you come to Me with your attitude being one of gratefulness and repentance, I will reassure you of My great love for you, and I will lead you through the fires of doubt and destruction that threaten to consume you.

"You will not be destroyed by the enemy's weapons, for I have placed a shield of protection around you. Stand firm in the truth of My Holy Word, and trust Me to deliver you from that which enslaves you."

2 Sam. 22:31 (NIV) ~ "As for God, his way is perfect: The Lord's word is flawless; he shields all who take refuge in him."

Me: "Lord, what do You want me to know today?"

God: "When I give you a certain task to carry out, believe that I will help you complete the work. Do not give up halfway through. Persevere to the end, and your efforts will bear much fruit. There will be no obstacles you and I can't overcome together. I will provide you with every tool you'll need to use, at the appropriate times.

"Remember that everything you do for My Name's sake will contribute to the entire kingdom work I am completing on this earth."

2 Chron. 15:7 (NIV) ~ "But as for you, be strong and do not give up, for your work will be rewarded."

Me: "Lord, what do You want me to know today?"

God: "Run to Me when your adversary is hounding you. My arms are outstretched, waiting to gather you in. You will not be taken in by his lies when you cling to the truths I have taught you.

"Let your words and actions speak of your faith in My constant guidance during your times of need. You will persevere through all that comes your way because you have called upon My Name and I have heard you. I will be your strength and your shield."

Ps. 28:7 (NIV) ~ "The Lord is my strength and my shield; my heart trusts in him, and he helps me. My heart leaps for joy, and with my song I praise him."

Me: "Lord, what do You want me to know today?"

God: "There will be situations in your life that are difficult to get through because you can't see what lies ahead. Remember that I am right here beside you, and I will lead you in the direction you need to go, in order that you may fulfill the purpose I've planted in your heart, even if you don't know yet what that is.

"Commune with Me. Ask Me to show you what your greatest purpose on this earth is. Listen for My voice. Read My Word and memorize it. Act upon every nudge I give you. Watch your greatest fears become your greatest triumphs. I will guide you and cheer you on, every step of the way. My best plans for you will mesh beautifully with your greatest dreams and desires when you entrust all of this into My care."

Is. 25:1 (NIV) ~ "Lord, you are my God; I will exalt you and praise your name, for in perfect faithfulness you have done wonderful things, things planned long ago."

Me: "Lord, what do You want me to know today?"

God: "Since I bought you with the blood of My Son, Jesus Christ, you are Mine. Yet, I have given you a free will to choose whether or not you will serve Me with all your heart and with gratitude for all you've been given. When you realize your life is not your own, it will be easier for you to submit to Me in those areas where you feel pulled in more than one direction.

"I have the best plan for your life. Will you trust Me to give you far greater blessings than you could ever create for yourself in your lifetime? Hold out your hands and receive what I will give you. You will not look back with regret."

1 Sam. 12:24 (NIV) ~ "But be sure to fear the Lord and serve him faithfully with all your heart; consider what great things he has done for you."

Me: "Lord, what do You want me to know today?"

God: "Seeing things through My eyes will give you a different perspective on life. Ask Me to show you those things that are important to Me in your life. Then, ask Me for guidance, that you may know what it is that I've created for you, specifically, to carry out in these areas.

"I will delight in showing you how valuable your efforts are, as you offer back to Me the best of your abilities for My kingdom purpose on earth."

Is. 48:17 (NIV) ~ "This is what the Lord says—your Redeemer, the Holy One of Israel: 'I am the Lord your God, who teaches you what is best for you, who directs you in the way you should go."

Me: "Lord, what do You want me to know today?"

God: "What will it benefit you to embrace the world and its charms? Nothing you truly desire will be found in the pursuit of worldly pleasures.

"Instead, chase after My heart above all else, and I will reveal to you My greatest wonders and most amazing joys that will uphold you through every trial you face in the coming days. You will see how precious your life really is when you look at it through My eyes."

Rom. 12:2 (NIV) ~ "Do not conform to the pattern of this world, but be transformed by the renewing of your mind. Then you will be able to test and approve what God's will is—his good, pleasing and perfect will."

Me: "Lord, what do You want me to know today?"

God: "What seems like an insurmountable hurdle to you is actually My hand at work creating something beautiful out of those circumstances you feel are a total waste of your valuable time. When you let go of whatever you are trying to control in your own strength, you will begin to feel a peace about letting Me take the lead to show you the direction I know will bring you the most joy and satisfaction, while enabling you to fulfill your greatest purpose on this earth at the same time. Follow Me, even when you can't see where I'm taking you. The journey will be amazing."

Eph. 3:20-21 (NIV) ~ "Now to him who is able to do immeasurably more than all we ask or imagine, according to his power that is at work within us, to him be glory in the church and in Christ Jesus throughout all generations, for ever and ever! Amen."

Me: "Lord, what do You want me to know today?"

God: "Where there are things you cannot control, there are answers being worked out by My hand. Watch what I will do with all that you've entrusted to Me. There will be every reason to rejoice in the end results."

Ps. 5:11 (NIV) ~ "But let all who take refuge in you be glad; let them ever sing for joy. Spread your protection over them, that those who love your name may rejoice in you."

Me: "Lord, what do You want me to know today?"

God: "I am preparing you for what lies ahead. There will be days when you can't feel Me present in your life. Those will be days when I am stretching your faith through circumstances that will make you stronger, as you rely on what I've already taught you and put your faith into action. In those situations, you will be a powerful witness for My Kingdom—a testimony of a life fully surrendered to Me."

Is. 40:31 (NIV) ~ "but those who hope in the Lord will renew their strength. They will soar on wings like eagles; they will run and not grow weary, they will walk and not be faint."

Me: "Lord, what do You want me to know today?"

God: "When it seems to you like you've come to a dead end regarding the direction for your future, that is when I am preparing you for a journey that will require your full trust in Me. I will pave a new path for you when it is time for you to move forward.

"By keeping your eyes and heart focused on Me, you won't miss the signs I will put in place to direct you toward the best destination you could ever imagine—one that will delight you and honor Me."

Ps. 119:35 (NIV) ~ "Direct me in the path of your commands, for there I find delight."

Me: "Lord, what do You want me to know today?"

God: "A willing heart and a contrite spirit are necessary for those who desire to walk closely with Me. The things I will share with you cannot be received and understood by anyone who refuses to acknowledge My authority over all heaven and earth. Heed My instruction in every area of your life, and do not let go of My hand when you feel at odds with where I am leading you.

"There will be no reason to question My guidance, for I have already proven to you in many ways your tremendous worth to Me—the greatest of these being the gift of salvation through the blood of My Son, Jesus Christ, being poured out for you at the cross. The resurrection of your Savior is all you need to remember when the going gets rough—how the love that raised Christ from the dead is also at work in your life right now. You are My child. I will be with you always."

Is. 66:2 (NIV) ~ "Has not my hand made all these things, and so they came into being?" declares the Lord. "These are the ones I look on with favor: those who are humble and contrite in spirit, and who tremble at my word."

Me: "Lord, what do You want me to know today?"

God: "Before time began, I knew you. I knew how you would respond to My love. I knew what would delight you, and what would motivate you to become the person I created you to be.

"You have the choice to either forge ahead into the unknown with faith in My sure guidance, or to stubbornly hold back until all the pieces of your future are in place as you feel they should be. If you do things your own way, you will miss out on the most wonderful blessings I have for you. Come, let Me show you the greatest treasures I have created for you to discover as you walk with Me daily."

2 Cor. 9:8 (NIV) ~ "And God is able to bless you abundantly, so that in all things at all times, having all that you need, you will abound in every good work."

Me: "Lord, what do You want me to know today?"

God: "As you focus on Me, through prayer and reading My Word, I will do a work in your heart that will give you more understanding of Who I am. I will reveal My heart to you in such a way that you will know without a doubt how much I love you.

"Do not hesitate to share with Me your deepest feelings —those doubts, fears, and seeming failures that plague you endlessly. I want to release you from those burdens and replace them with confidence that I have a wonderful plan for your life—a plan that was created just for you. You must not compare yourself to others, for you are uniquely you. Knowing there is no one else exactly like you gives you the freedom to be yourself. Take joy in that, and encourage others to find their God-given strengths and to use them for My glory. We are on this journey together. I will show you that your best days are still to come."

Ps. 62:8 (NIV) ~ "Trust in him at all times, you people; pour out your hearts to him, for God is our refuge."

Me: "Lord, what do You want me to know today?"

God: "I have been working out the details of your life in ways you can't always recognize. When you think about all you've been through and the people who have crossed your path along the way, you will find numerous blessings to count.

"Some situations you go through are not for your benefit, but someone else's, that they may sense My Presence at work in their life as they process what you are going through. Be willing to face hard trials when they come, for there will be a good purpose for the pain involved, and you will see My provision for you in many forms as you trust Me to walk you through the fire. No need of yours will go unmet, though My answers may look different than what you expect."

James 1:2-4 (NIV) ~ "Consider it pure joy, my brothers and sisters, whenever you face trials of many kinds, because you know that the testing of your faith produces perseverance. Let perseverance finish its work so that you may be mature and complete, not lacking anything."

Me: "Lord, what do You want me to know today?"

God: "Rise up and listen to My plans for you. I have given you more than enough reasons to never doubt Me when I call upon you to carry out what I've given you to do.

"Now, let go of those things that hinder you from moving forward, and latch onto that which will produce good fruit in your life, so that others may see and know that I am God. Compare yourself to no one, for you have been given what only you can complete for My kingdom's purpose."

John 15:2 (NIV) ~ "He cuts off every branch in me that bears no fruit, while every branch that does bear fruit he prunes so that it will be even more fruitful."

Me: "Lord, what do You want me to know today?"

God: "I have been at work in your heart, thanks to your prayers and the prayers of others. When you see and recognize Me at work in your life situations, do not hesitate to embrace what I am doing and lean into Me for the comfort and support you need. I will turn your mourning into dancing, and I will show you how much I love you through all the ways I interact with you; pay attention to My signals. You will be encouraged more and more as you learn to recognize the ways I am communicating with you through My Holy Word.

"When I work out details in your life that you know can only happen through My Divine intervention, you will have no doubt about My desire to lead you every step of the way on your journey through this life. Your dreams and My perfect plans for you will be seamlessly interwoven into a masterpiece that we will both delight in one day."

Jer. 29:11 (NIV) ~ "For I know the plans I have for you, declares the Lord, plans to prosper you and not to harm you, plans to give you hope and a future."

Me: "Lord, what do You want me to know today?"

God: "When I make known to you those things I want you to accomplish for My kingdom purpose, I will also provide all you need, in order that you can complete the tasks I've set before you. Do not hesitate to move forward in faith when I urge you to do so. You will see My hand at work alongside you, and you will be encouraged even as you encourage others through your diligent acts of obedience to Me.

"Your life will have greater purpose when you serve others with a heart of thanksgiving, thinking not about what it will cost you in the end. I will always give you enough: enough time, enough patience, enough ability, enough wisdom, enough love to share with another who is in need. Trust Me to go before you to open doors when necessary. Your job is to obey—keep moving. We've got this!"

2 Thess. 3:16 (NIV) ~ "Now may the Lord of peace himself give you peace at all times and in every way. The Lord be with all of you."

Me: "Lord, what do You want me to know today?"

God: "When the reason for your restlessness becomes overwhelming, remember that I am here with arms open wide to receive you and to lighten your burden. I will carry you through every valley you come to. Though there be giants in your life, you will not be defeated. I will fight for you."

Matt. 11:28 (NIV) ~ "Come to me, all you who are weary and burdened, and I will give you rest."

Me: "Lord, what do You want me to know today?"

God: "Let go of that which you hold so tightly to—the things that keep you so absorbed with yourself and your pursuit of personal happiness. Release those things to Me, and let Me reconstruct your life into one of immeasurable value and purpose that will pour over into the lives of others in so many tangible ways.

"I created you with unique gifts and talents that were meant to be shared in ways I will show you when you ask for My help—take delight in this. Your purpose on earth has far-reaching capabilities. Don't shortchange yourself and miss out on the opportunities I've created just for you. Many lives will be blessed through your obedience to Me."

Prov. 19:21 (NIV) ~ "Many are the plans in a person's heart, but it is the Lord's purpose that prevails."

Me: "Lord, what do You want me to know today?"

God: "Sometimes, you will feel inadequate for the situations I place you in and the responsibilities I hand over to you. That's okay. Just trust Me to give you the wisdom and strength you'll need as you move forward one step at a time. You will see that I've created in you more capability and tenacity to survive and thrive than you ever thought possible.

"As you lean on Me for support, you will feel My love empowering you in every area you need it. Never resist a chance to be stretched in your faith, for I am doing a tremendous work in your life. When I ask you to take a leap of faith, always remember that I will be here to catch you and rejoice with you. Some who are watching you need to see your vulnerability in this area. Be willing to be transparent, that others may know I am the reason for your joy, your peace, and your strength."

Ps. 143:8 (NIV) ~ "Let the morning bring me word of your unfailing love, for I have put my trust in you. Show me the way I should go, for to you I entrust my life."

Me: "Lord, what do You want me to know today?"

God: "Where I have placed you in this season of your life is where I want you to use your gifts and talents for My kingdom purpose. There will be many distractions that come your way, but if you keep your focus directed on what I've given you to do it will consistently become easier for you to say 'no' to those things that have little or no value in your life when compared to the riches of My blessings.

"Take joy in all you do for My Name's sake, and the harvest you reap will be plentiful."

Ps. 1:3 (NIV) ~ "That person is like a tree planted by streams of water, which yields its fruit in season and whose leaf does not wither—whatever they do prospers."

Me: "Lord, what do You want me to know today?"

God: "Take the time to evaluate those situations in your life that come between you and I. Where do your motives conflict with what you know I expect of you?

"When you let Me lead you in the direction I know is right for you, there will be no other scenario that will bring you greater joy. You will learn to recognize and embrace My truths that apply to your specific situations, and you will be able to overcome those doubts and fears that hold you back from completing your purpose on this earth. Trust Me to keep you grounded in the right areas, as you lean on Me for guidance and strength."

Ps. 25:5 (NIV) ~ "Guide me in your truth and teach me, for you are God my Savior, and my hope is in you all day long."

Me: "Lord, what do You want me to know today?"

God: "Where there is a need to be met, I will provide the people and resources to do the job. If I lay it on your heart to be praying for someone, then that is the most important thing you can do to help them until I tell you otherwise.

"Do not slack in your prayers for others, because the power of prayer in Jesus' Name is immeasurable, and this is one of the most urgent jobs I'll ever give you. You have no idea how much the prayers of others, on your behalf, have affected your life situations. Never doubt that every prayer you utter will be heard by Me and answered according to My perfect plan for everyone involved."

Eph. 6:18 (NIV) ~ "And pray in the Spirit on all occasions with all kinds of prayers and requests. With this in mind, be alert and always keep on praying for all the Lord's people."

Me: "Lord, what do You want me to know today?"

God: "Speak to Me about every concern on your heart, and tell Me those things you could never tell another person. I care about every detail of your life—past, present, and future. When you trust Me enough that you would willingly expose every vulnerable part of your heart to Me for examination, then you will know My perfect peace. For though nothing can be hidden from Me, when you freely offer all you hold onto into My safekeeping, I will bless this act of faith on your part.

"Practice this regularly, and you will learn how freeing it is to walk with Me and commune closely with Me each day. Your burdens will become lighter, and your joy will be full."

Ps. 51:17 (NIV) ~ "My sacrifice, O God, is a broken spirit; a broken and contrite heart you, God, will not despise."

Me: "Lord, what do You want me to know today?"

God: "My plans for you are always better than your plans because I see the whole picture of your life at this very moment. Ask Me to direct your path, and I will. Can you see even one day ahead, to what will happen tomorrow? When you trust Me with all of your days and seek My will for the rest of your life, you shall know peace in your heart, unlike anything the world can give you.

"When you use your gifts and talents in ways that honor Me, I will turn these offerings into blessings that will enrich the lives of many other people besides yourself. You have no idea how I will multiply your efforts when you put Me first in the equation of your daily goals."

Ps. 33:11 (NIV) ~ "But the plans of the Lord stand firm forever, the purposes of his heart through all generations."

Me: "Lord, what do You want me to know today?"

God: "I am with you at all times. When you reach out to Me in times of need, I will hear the cry of your heart, and I will reassure you when you falter in your faith in My timing.

"No prayer of yours will go unanswered. I love you, and I will use your specific situation as a tool with which I will teach you all you need to know about the practice of unwavering faith in your Heavenly Father's ability to handle anything you face."

Phil. 4:6-7 (NIV) ~ "Do not be anxious about anything, but in every situation, by prayer and petition, with thanksgiving, present your requests to God. And the peace of God, which transcends all understanding, will guard your hearts and your minds in Christ Jesus."

Me: "Lord, what do You want me to know today?"

God: "Whatever you face today, remember that I have given you the strength to overcome all obstacles that seem overwhelming to you. By the power of My Holy Name, you can do more than you ever thought possible. Call upon Me, and I will supply all you need for the trials that lie ahead. There will be no room for defeat in your day when you grasp My hand and feel My love holding you up."

Col. 1:11 (NIV) ~ "being strengthened with all power according to his glorious might so that you may have great endurance and patience,"

Me: "Lord, what do You want me to know today?"

God: "I have given you My Words of Life, in the Holy Bible. As you read from My Word each day, you will come to know My heart more deeply and clearly. You will have more ability to share My love with others, and you will sense Me working in your heart the more you fill it with My truth.

"I created you with a desire to worship. If you are not worshiping Me, first and foremost, then you are filling that void with something of the world. Ask Me to give you a heart of worship for Me alone. Stay grounded in My Word and in prayer. When you do these things, I will give you a peace that passes understanding, and you will be an encouragement to others as you share with them the reason for your hope."

Ps. 119:105 (NIV) ~ "Your word is a lamp to my feet and a light for my path."

Me: "Lord, what do You want me to know today?"

God: "Stand up for what you know is right. Do not let just a few faithful people bear the cross for My Name's sake.

"When I give you an opportunity to speak My truth into someone's life, do it. Don't wait, hoping someone else will fill your role. You have been placed right where you are for such a time as this. Look beyond your own comfort and be a light for a hurting soul, that they may see and know that I am God."

Rom. 1:16 (NIV) ~ "For I am not ashamed of the gospel, because it is the power of God that brings salvation to everyone who believes: first to the Jew, then to the Gentile."

Me: "Lord, what do You want me to know today?"

God: "I have given you more blessings than you can count. Let My blessings be a reminder to you of how much I love you.

"I am working out My purpose for you even now. Trust Me with your heart wide open, and I will fill it with more of My truth, more of My love, and with the discernment you will need to navigate the route that lies ahead. There will be nothing you and I can't conquer together."

Ps. 34:8 (NIV) ~ "Taste and see that the Lord is good; blessed is the one who takes refuge in him."

April 21

Me: "Lord, what do You want me to know today?"

God: "I can see where you're headed and whether your choices will produce fruit for My Kingdom or not. Keep asking Me for wisdom and discernment in all things you do, and I will keep you moving in the right direction.

"Let your motivation be that of a child of the King, for that is who you are. I am training you to represent My Kingdom to the fullest of your ability. I will give you responsibilities that will grow you in your relationship with Me. I will also give you opportunities to use your gifts and talents in such a way as to be an encouragement to others, and as a confirmation to you of all I've entrusted you with."

Ps. 119:125 (NIV) ~ "I am your servant; give me discernment that I may understand your statutes."

Me: "Lord, what do You want me to know today?"

God: "There will be times when you want to give up because you don't see My direction clearly. I am still right here with you, and I am orchestrating your circumstances so that when you take the next step in faith, there will be timely encouragement that will propel you to keep moving to the next level.

"Even when you do not visibly see progress taking place, I am at work laying the foundation ahead of you, upon which your faithful acts of stewardship for My kingdom purpose will be built and will flourish under My watchful guidance."

Heb. 11:1 (NIV) ~ "Now faith is confidence in what we hope for and assurance about what we do not see."

Me: "Lord, what do You want me to know today?"

God: "Remember that I've given you a unique purpose to carry out in your lifetime. Your distinct purpose is unlike that of anyone else on earth. There will be those who don't understand why you're doing what you do, but I created you for this specific reason—that you might be an extension of My own heart when you use your gifts and talents to reflect your love for Me and My creation."

Prov. 27:19 (NIV) ~ "As water reflects the face, so one's life reflects the heart."

Me: "Lord, what do You want me to know today?"

God: "Caring for others is a way you can show My love to them. Reach out in whatever way I nudge you and be My light in someone's life today. Remember what it feels like to be on the receiving end of such love; let that be your motivation."

Is. 58:10 (NIV) ~ "and if you spend yourselves in behalf of the hungry and satisfy the needs of the oppressed, then your light will rise in the darkness, and your night will become like the noonday."

Me: "Lord, what do You want me to know today?"

God: "What will you do with the rest of your life? Will you spend it as one who can't see the future yet plods along consistently in blind faith, believing I will guide you and direct you at all times, or will you spend it running around in circles, blind to the truths I have shown you and the wisdom I have imparted to you through so many sources over the years?

"There's still time to finish well. Do not give up and do not give in—I'm right here beside you for the journey. Stay the course, and I will refill your cup as needed. Just keep moving forward. Trust Me in all things. I will be your Strength."

Ps. 119:60 (NIV) ~ "I will hasten and not delay to obey your commands."

Me: "Lord, what do You want me to know today?"

God: "There will come a time when all that you struggle with now will be behind you. I am giving you the strength you need as you need it so that you are able to claim victory over each battle you face every day, big or small. Run to Me in good times and bad. Let Me rejoice with you when the spectacular takes your breath away, and let Me comfort you when disaster knocks the wind out of you.

"When you look back at your life's journey one day, you will see all I've brought you through. Even though you don't understand the reason for your trials right now, believe I am working things out with an eternal purpose in mind—something far-reaching and far greater than you can imagine. Your life is a story of My love and faithfulness, that others may see and know that I am God. Be encouraged."

Ex. 15:2 (NIV) ~ "The Lord is my strength and my defense; he has become my salvation. He is my God, and I will praise him, my father's God, and I will exalt him."

Me: "Lord, what do You want me to know today?"

God: "When you realize how full your cup of blessings is and has been for all of your life, you will feel more appreciation for what I am doing in the midst of your struggles right now. I am creating in you a stunning transformation of the heart as you cooperate with Me more and more in the hard areas—those areas of your life that no one else sees.

"As you loosen your grip on those things you try so desperately to control yourself, you will have more peace of mind as I show you how even the hardest things you deal with can be turned around into something beautiful that will minister to others when you allow Me to be fully involved in the whole process."

Eccl. 3:11 (NIV) ~ "He has made everything beautiful in its time. He has also set eternity in the human heart; yet no one can fathom what God has done from beginning to end."

Me: "Lord, what do You want me to know today?"

God: "Wherever there is cause for concern in your life, I am working out a solution. You needn't worry over what you can't control. I am outside of time; I see the whole picture. There is always room for more faith in your heart. As you reflect on what I've done in your life thus far, you will no doubt come to realize that I've been more involved than you thought.

"Keep talking to Me about everything that crosses your mind; give it all over to Me and see what I will do. There is no need for you to carry a heavy burden—that's what I'm here for. Lean on Me, and I will be your strength, always."

Ps. 86:11 (NIV) ~ "Teach me your way, Lord, that I may rely on your faithfulness; give me an undivided heart, that I may fear your name."

Me: "Lord, what do You want me to know today?"

God: "There is one who seeks to destroy you. He is the father of lies. Do not listen to anything he whispers in your ear. You have been bought with the blood of the Lamb. Your life is not your own. You will recognize My voice by the peace that comes with obeying what I've told you. The enemy cannot give you peace, for it is not in him."

John 14:27 (NIV) ~ "Peace I leave with you; my peace I give you. I do not give to you as the world gives. Do not let your hearts be troubled and do not be afraid."

Me: "Lord, what do You want me to know today?"

God: "My will for you will always be that you would seek Me first over all else. Do not let your heart become crowded with useless distractions that will blur your spiritual vision. My purpose for your life includes joy overflowing, but within the context of your full obedience to Me.

"You have no idea of the heights My love will take you to as you give Me the full reign of your heart. Let Me show you the extent of what you were created for."

Matt. 6:33 (NIV) ~ "But seek first his kingdom and his righteousness, and all these things will be given to you as well."

Me: "Lord, what do You want me to know today?"

God: "Set your sights on things above, not on things of this world. I have given you so much to be thankful for. You need only look around you to see your blessings—they are everywhere, yet what you see with your physical eyes are things that will not last. Open your spiritual eyes to see those blessings that are eternal; take time to list them and be grateful for each one."

Col. 3:2 (NIV) ~ "Set your minds on things above, not on earthly things."

Me: "Lord, what do You want me to know today?"

God: "When I created you, I had a specific purpose in mind; I have shown you some of that purpose through the gifts and talents I've given you, and I've left some to be discovered by you as you seek to know Me better.

"When you know who you are in Christ, you will understand more of whom I've created you to be. Then, as you fulfill the purpose I've given you while walking closely with Me, hand-in-hand, you will experience a joy like nothing the world has to offer, and you will know without a doubt how much I love you."

Phil. 2:13 (NIV) ~ "for it is God who works in you to will and to act in order to fulfill his good purpose."

Me: "Lord, what do You want me to know today?"

God: "When you come to Me with a request, leave it in My care and proceed with your day. Do not waste a single moment worrying or doubting whether I will hear you and answer you. Your request will be taken care of in My perfect timing. All you need to be concerned with is whether or not you are using the abilities I've given you to carry out My purpose in your life."

James 1:6 (NIV) ~ "But when you ask, you must believe and not doubt, because the one who doubts is like a wave of the sea, blown and tossed by the wind."

May 4

Me: "Lord, what do You want me to know today?"

God: "There will be times when you won't be able to accomplish your goals in your own strength. That's because I want you to lean on Me. I want to show you a better way to go about completing what I've put in your heart to do.

"I will let you make your own plans, but until you acknowledge My sovereignty in your life, you will expend much energy on things that will prove fruitless in the end when compared to the value of every effort spent pursuing My will and My grand purpose, created explicitly for you to fulfill in your lifetime. Don't miss out on the best I still have in store for you."

Deut. 4:39 (NIV) ~ "Acknowledge and take to heart this day that the Lord is God in heaven above and on the earth below. There is no other."

Me: "Lord, what do You want me to know today?"

God: "How many times have you seen My hand inter-vene in your life to rescue you from situations that might have been harmful to you? Even when you are not aware of it, I am guarding you from all kinds of affliction—physical, emotional, and spiritual. I love you more than you know."

Ps. 5:11 (NIV) ~ "But let all who take refuge in you be glad; let them ever sing for joy. Spread your protection over them, that those who love your name may rejoice in you."

Me: "Lord, what do You want me to know today?"

God: "When you fervently seek My will for your life, My answers to your questions will be made clear for you to understand. As you wait to hear from Me, keep your eyes focused on those things that will remind you of My love for you, so you will not doubt that I am indeed working out your present situation, as well as your future. The better you know Me, the more peace you will experience as your faith in My sovereignty continues to grow."

Ps. 105:4 (NIV) ~ "Look to the Lord and his strength; seek his face always."

Me: "Lord, what do You want me to know today?"

God: "I am producing in you good fruit for My kingdom purpose on earth. Be willing to be pruned when necessary, for this will ensure the maximum yield I have created in you to be produced for My glory. When you see how abundant your life will be, in accordance with My plans for you, your cup of joy will run over into the lives of the people I've placed all around you.

"Do not listen to the lies of the enemy when he tries to poison every new area of growth that I've been nourishing in your heart. You were made to thrive with everything that I've poured into you, and by all that you've offered up to Me in surrender."

John 15:8 (NIV) ~ "This is to my Father's glory, that you bear much fruit, showing yourselves to be my disciples."

Me: "Lord, what do You want me to know today?"

God: "My child, when you call to Me in prayer, I will always be here listening to the cries of your heart. Your every prayer will be answered according to My perfect plan for your life. I care about everything that matters to you. The more you talk with Me, the more of Myself I will reveal to you through My answers to your prayers. Trust Me to get it right."

Ps. 3:4 (NIV) ~ "I call out to the Lord, and he answers me from his holy mountain."

Me: "Lord, what do You want me to know today?"

God: "When the voices of doubt creep into your thoughts, dismiss them immediately by reciting truths from My Word. I have given you the ability to be an overcomer and a victor in every circumstance that threatens to defeat you. When you can't see the way to move forward and out of a situation you are in at any given time, I will show you another way to look at it, which will clearly lead you in the direction you need to go.

"Always come to Me first; then you can confidently move forward, knowing I will direct your path in such a way that you will never lose your footing. Your journey with Me will be sure and steadfast, and full of good purpose throughout your lifetime."

Ps. 119:133 (NIV) ~ "Direct my footsteps according to your word; let no sin rule over me."

Me: "Lord, what do You want me to know today?"

God: "Grasp hold of the very things that cause you to stumble in your walk with Me, and lay them down at My feet in surrender. I will replace them with treasures that man cannot supply, from the abundance of My provision for you. You will find that you truly have no need for those things that rob you of precious time, energy, and peace of mind.

"Concentrate on what I've instilled upon your heart for you to do, and you will experience a joy that extends into eternity as you carry out My will on earth."

Ps. 119:165 (NIV) ~ "Great peace have those who love your law, and nothing can make them stumble."

Me: "Lord, what do You want me to know today?"

God: "Sometimes there will be no quick answer to your prayers—this does not mean I'm not listening to you; it simply means I have a greater purpose being worked out, which will benefit a number of people besides yourself, and this will take time to complete.

"Trust Me to set in motion every action needed at the perfect time to fulfill My answer to your prayers. You need only to trust Me in all things, at all times."

Ps. 9:10 (NIV) ~ "Those who know your name trust in you, for you, Lord, have never forsaken those who seek you."

Me: "Lord, what do You want me to know today?"

God: "There is nothing more sure than My love for you. Don't hesitate to call on My Name in any and every situation you find yourself in. I will be with you always, and there will be no reason for fear to overtake you because I am in charge of all things. Nothing happens without Me allowing it. Therefore, ask for My peace, and you shall have it, even as you trust Me to work all things out in My perfect timing."

Ps. 31:7 (NIV) ~ "I will be glad and rejoice in your love, for you saw my affliction and knew the anguish of my soul."

Me: "Lord, what do You want me to know today?"

God: "I have made you for My pleasure. I put a song in your heart that only you can sing; sing it well. Encourage others also to sing their song, i.e., use their gifts and talents for My glory, and you will see how your passion for shining the light of Christ will ignite other souls with a holy purpose that will spread like wildfire through generations to come. Never underestimate what I can accomplish through your one willing heart, offered for My service."

Ps. 40:3 (NIV) ~ "He put a new song in my mouth, a hymn of praise to our God. Many will see and fear the Lord and put their trust in him."

Me: "Lord, what do You want me to know today?"

God: "Rebellious hearts lead people astray. Always seek to be one who listens for My voice and heeds My warnings. When you ask Me for help, with a sincere heart, I will hear you and will answer. You needn't concern yourself with trying to figure everything out; just trust and obey."

Deut. 32:1 (NIV) ~ "Listen, you heavens, and I will speak; hear, you earth, the words of my mouth."

Me: "Lord, what do You want me to know today?"

God: "There is one who seeks to destroy your devotion to Me. He is the father of lies; do not listen to his divisive schemes. Instead, listen to and obey My Voice of Truth, the Holy Spirit living in you. He will guide and direct you in the way you should go."

John 14:26 (NIV) ~ "But the Advocate, the Holy Spirit, whom the Father will send in my name, will teach you all things and will remind you of everything I have said to you."

Me: "Lord, what do You want me to know today?"

God: "With certainty, I am carrying out My good purpose in your life. There will be nothing that can hinder the blessings I have for you when you walk hand-in-hand with Me. Just as surely as the morning sun rises in the east, so shall My love carry you through anything that comes your way.

"When you have doubts, hand them right over to Me, and I will reassure you of My ability to transform your doubts into faith in My all-sustaining provision for you."

Is. 46:4 (NIV) ~ "Even to your old age and gray hairs I am he, I am he who will sustain you. I have made you and I will carry you; I will sustain you and I will rescue you."

Me: "Lord, what do You want me to know today?"

God: "There will be cause for an examination of your heart on a daily basis. Do not neglect this practice, for it is vital to the health of your relationship with Me. When I nudge you to take notice of your thoughts and actions, do so immediately. Then, act upon what you know is right and acceptable in My sight."

Prov. 8:32 (NIV) ~ "Now then, my children, listen to me; blessed are those who keep my ways."

Me: "Lord, what do You want me to know today?"

God: "My hand will be upon you in protection when the enemy strikes with devious plans. You need never fear what you cannot see coming, for I am going ahead of you to make clear the path I want you to follow. Stay grounded in My Word, and in prayer and fellowship with Me. Then you will know the peace that only I can give you when everything around you seems chaotic."

Ps. 29:11 (NIV) ~ "The Lord gives strength to his people; the Lord blesses his people with peace."

Me: "Lord, what do You want me to know today?"

God: "Whether or not you see tangible answers to your prayers, I am working on them, and they are being constructed in such a way that they will produce fruit for My Kingdom in your life and the lives of others you pray for.

"Never stop praying for every need you know of, for it is My delight to hear and answer your every plea, no matter how large or small it may seem to you. You have no idea how often your prayers have moved mountains in someone's life, or how many trials you have been spared from because of someone else interceding for you in prayer. Do not underestimate the great power of this tool I've given you."

1 Thess. 5:16-18 (NIV) ~ "Rejoice always, pray continually, give thanks in all circumstances; for this is God's will for you in Christ Jesus."

Me: "Lord, what do You want me to know today?"

God: "I am the Alpha and the Omega, the Beginning and the End. I see every day of your life, every breath you've taken and all those yet to come. I have an exact purpose for you right now, right where you are on your life's journey. Trust Me to provide all you need as you simply put one foot in front of the other and move forward, holding My hand."

Ps. 139:16 (NIV) ~ "Your eyes saw my unformed body; all the days ordained for me were written in your book before one of them came to be."

Me: "Lord, what do You want me to know today?"

God: "Why harbor doubts in your heart regarding your future? I have all the answers you'll need. Just follow Me in the direction I lead you, and you will see how everything will turn out in a way that points to My everlasting love for you. There is nothing I can't accomplish in your life when you let Me be your Guiding Light."

Heb. 10:23 (NIV) ~ "Let us hold unswervingly to the hope we profess, for he who promised is faithful."

Me: "Lord, what do You want me to know today?"

God: "Long before there was any sign of My purpose in your life, I laid out the plans I have for you. I designed you to bring Me glory in a way that is unique to your particular giftedness and personality. Allow Me to guide you along the path I have set for you. There will be opportunities to stretch your faith and abilities along the way. I delight in walking closely with you as you discover all the blessings I've planned for your journey."

Ps. 16:11 (NIV) ~ "You make known to me the path of life; you will fill me with joy in your presence, with eternal pleasures at your right hand."

Me: "Lord, what do You want me to know today?"

God: "There is nothing you will face today that I haven't already seen coming. I will be your strength in every situation. Commit your day to My safekeeping and trust Me in all things. There will be blessings for you to discover; keep your eyes open. The love of the world can never compare to My love for you."

2 Sam. 22:33 (NIV) ~ "It is God who arms me with strength and keeps my way secure."

Me: "Lord, what do You want me to know today?"

God: "See to it that you practice daily those things I've given you to do that will reflect Me and My kingdom work in your life. By concentrating your efforts on these particular things, you will know a sense of purpose that will keep you focused on the One Who assigned them to you, which translates into living an abundant life."

Col. 3:23 (NIV) ~ "Whatever you do, work at it with all your heart, as working for the Lord, not for human masters,"

Me: "Lord, what do You want me to know today?"

God: "Keep looking to Me for wisdom and discernment. Call on My Name throughout your day. I will hear you and will direct your ways as you lean on Me. When you feel overwhelmed, remember the victories I've given you previously, and trust Me to walk you through whatever comes your way."

1 Cor. 15:57 (NIV) ~ "But thanks be to God! He gives us the victory through our Lord Jesus Christ."

Me: "Lord, what do You want me to know today?"

God: "When the time comes for you to know My will for your future, it will be revealed to you. Keep moving forward, and I will steer you in the direction you should go. Follow My lead, and I will teach you new things about yourself and others that will be relevant to where I am taking you on your life's journey."

Acts 2:28 (NIV) ~ "You have made known to me the paths of life; you will fill me with joy in your presence."

Me: "Lord, what do You want me to know today?"

God: "See how I am at work in your circumstances; take notice of changes as they occur. Thank Me in the good times and the bad times, for I am working out the puzzle of your life, putting the pieces together in the right places at the right times. The end result will be a stunning picture of a life lived victoriously and surrendered at the same time, with My fingerprints all over it.

"When you surrendered your heart to Christ Jesus as your Savior, you became victorious in Him, cleansed by His blood shed for you at Calvary. Now, live each day as one who has been given new life. Let your joy be contagious so others may know My great love for them, also."

1 Chron. 29:13 (NIV) ~ "Now, our God, we give you thanks, and praise your glorious name."

Me: "Lord, what do You want me to know today?"

God: "There is one who would like nothing more than to see you fail in your walk with Me—this is your enemy, the wicked foe. He will stop at nothing in his attempt to destroy the advancement of My Kingdom on earth. I have given you the ability, as My child, to use prayer in the Name of Jesus as a powerful weapon to defeat the enemy when he attacks. Believe I will hear your prayers and act upon them. You will see victories in areas you never thought possible when you pray with an unrelenting diligence and with faith in My sovereign power and wisdom."

Ps. 17:6 (NIV) ~ "I call on you, my God, for you will answer me; turn your ear to me and hear my prayer."

Me: "Lord, what do You want me to know today?"

God: "Make it your life's purpose to seek ways in which you can use your gifts and talents for not only your own enjoyment but also for encouraging others and sharing My love with them in tangible ways. When you allow Me to direct your paths and projects, I will show you how even the smallest act of love toward another person, who will benefit from your particular generosity, will change a life in such a way that it will reverberate through generations to come.

"Don't live your days selfishly, but instead watch for and act upon every opportunity I give you to bless others, even as I have blessed you."

Phil. 2:3-4 (NIV) ~ "Do nothing out of selfish ambition or vain conceit. Rather, in humility value others above yourselves, not looking to your own interests but each of you to the interests of the others."

Me: "Lord, what do You want me to know today?"

God: "Learn from your past mistakes, and move forward with all faith in My timing and direction for your future. When one door closes, I will open another one for you, which will lead you toward the next adventure I am taking you on—one that will require your full attention to be focused on listening to the voice of your Heavenly Father and doing as I instruct you. Don't doubt that I have already laid out a perfect plan for you. Just trust and obey."

Ps. 31:3 (NIV) ~ "Since you are my rock and my fortress, for the sake of your name lead and guide me."

"Me: "Lord, what do You want me to know today?"

God: "You are secure in My love. You have given your heart to Me, and I am shaping it, molding it, refining it to be more like My own. Just as a child looks to their earthly father for wisdom and direction, I am training you, My child, in the way you should go.

"Do not swerve to the left or the right, but keep your eyes on Me and I will continue to lead you in the way ever-lasting. There is nothing in your path that I won't lead you through. I will never leave you nor forsake you. Lean on Me, and I will hold you up."

Ps. 37:23-24 (NIV) ~ "The Lord makes firm the steps of the one who delights in him; though he may stumble, he will not fall, for the Lord upholds him with his hand."

Me: "Lord, what do You want me to know today?"

God: "Look to My Word for the answers you seek. Everything you need to know is found in the Holy Bible. Do not be intimidated by the vastness of knowledge found there. I will show you what I want you to learn when you open the pages of My Word and begin reading, asking Me for understanding and direction.

"As you grow in your understanding of Who I am and what I want to teach you, you will also grow in your faith in Me, and you will see unmistakable evidence of My hand at work in your life right now."

Prov. 4:5 (NIV) ~ "Get wisdom, get understanding; do not forget my words or turn away from them."

June 2

Me: "Lord, what do You want me to know today?"

God: "Listen to everything I am telling you and apply it to your life, so that you may know the blessing of My favor upon you as you walk forward with Me in faith and integrity. There will be no shame for those who willingly obey My commands, but rather a heart filled with joy, and a peace that passes understanding."

John 14:23 (NIV) ~ "Jesus replied, 'Anyone who loves me will obey my teaching. My Father will love them, and we will come to them and make our home with them.'"

Me: "Lord, what do You want me to know today?"

God: "Anything I ask you to do will be something I've already empowered you to complete. All you need to remember is this: When you call upon My Name for help, I will be here. I will instruct you as you set one foot in front of the other on your journey of obedience to Me.

"Do not let your fears hold you back from experiencing the path I've prepared for you to travel on. You are safest when you are where I've planned for you to be at any given moment. Trust Me. I love you more than you can imagine."

Ps. 25:1 (NIV) ~ "In you, Lord my God, I put my trust."

Me: "Lord, what do You want me to know today?"

God: "Look no further than your own heart if you want to know what's wrong with this nation. Repentance begins right there. Call out to Me, and I will forgive you. Be the one willing to change, whether others follow suit or not. There are times when one simple act of obedience will spark a chain reaction that will eventually affect a far greater purpose at hand.

"Open your heart to what I want to accomplish through you in the days ahead. Ask Me to show you My will for you. I will open your eyes, that you may see what you've been missing while your focus was misdirected."

2 Cor. 7:10 (NIV) ~ "Godly sorrow brings repentance that leads to salvation and leaves no regret, but worldly sorrow brings death."

Me: "Lord, what do You want me to know today?"

God: "Let Me show you what real love is: Turn your eyes upon Jesus and bask in His presence daily. Fall on your knees before Him. Call out to Him in praise and worship. Repent of your sins and ask Him to forgive you. You've already asked Him to live in your heart, and He is there. Now, allow His love and mercy to wash over you and cleanse you as you rest quietly before Him. He will fill your empty places with a peace that passes understanding.

"Let Him have everything you hold onto; give it all over to Him. Trust Him with your deepest hurts and your wildest dreams. He died and rose again that you may have life and have it abundantly. Trust Jesus, as your Lord and Savior, to carry you through whatever comes your way. He will never leave you or forsake you."

1 John 4:9 (NIV) ~ "This is how God showed his love among us: He sent his one and only Son into the world that we might live through him."

Me: "Lord, what do You want me to know today?"

God: "Sometimes I let you go through hard things just to show you how resilient I created you to be. There is no one else on earth who will travel the same path you alone will take. Don't compare yourself to anyone else, but instead, be willing to be stretched and shaped into a better version of you as you lean on Me for strength and guidance every step of the way. You are My masterpiece. I know what you are capable of accomplishing and how I will help you get it done."

Ps. 59:16 (NIV) ~ "But I will sing of your strength, in the morning I will sing of your love; for you are my fortress, my refuge in times of trouble."

June 7

Me: "Lord, what do You want me to know today?"

God: "When you sense My Presence in your life, do not ignore Me. There are things I want to teach you and places I want to take you if you will let Me direct your path. Your plans and Mine will intersect beautifully when you let Me do the leading."

John 14:26 (NIV) ~ "But the Advocate, the Holy Spirit, whom the Father will send in my name, will teach you all things and will remind you of everything I have said to you."

Me: "Lord, what do You want me to know today?"

God: "Consistency is important in whatever you do relating to the purpose I've created you for—the gifts and talents I've given you, the people I've given you to love and care for, your own body which I've given you to live in and care for, and your relationship with Me (which affects every other aspect of your life). When you formulate a plan to manage these areas consistently, you will see success far greater than you imagined could happen. Your ability to profoundly affect the world around you will grow with each step forward you take— exercising self-discipline and practicing obedience to My leading.

"I have great things in store for you. Make sure you've done the necessary footwork to be ready for the joys and responsibilities I will hand over to you in the days ahead."

Luke 12:35-36 (NIV) ~ "Be dressed ready for service and keep your lamps burning, like servants waiting for their master to return from a wedding banquet, so that when he comes and knocks they can immediately open the door for him."

Me: "Lord, what do You want me to know today?"

God: "It matters not what the world says you should be doing at this point in your life, but rather, what your Heavenly Father has purposed for you to do. I will show you My plans for you when you readily seek My will and search for My signposts in your life. I have placed markers to direct your path, and they will become more visible to you when you learn to recognize the ways I am at work in your life.

"Your journey is unique to you. The way I speak to you will also be uniquely between you and Me. The more you get to know Me, the easier it will be for you to recognize and understand your Father's voice. You do not need to depend only on what I tell you through messages spoken by others, for I have so many things I want to share with you, specifically, as you and I commune together on a regular basis. Do not miss out on these treasured moments you and I will spend together. You will find them to be immeasurably priceless in value, and your life will be all the richer for it."

1 Chron. 16:10 (NIV) ~ "Glory in his holy name; let the hearts of those who seek the Lord rejoice."

Me: "Lord, what do You want me to know today?"

God: "I have shown you through My Word and through answers to your prayers that I am indeed very interested in being involved in your life, down to the tiniest detail. When you call on My Name, believing I have the power to hear you and answer, you are honoring Me as your God and Father. Let this be a regular practice in your life, a daily habit in your walk with Me.

"I want to be the first one you talk to about everything. You will see a positive change in the way you look at your circumstances in life when you share them with Me first, in prayer, before taking any other action to deal with them."

Heb. 4:16 (NIV) ~ "Let us then approach God's throne of grace with confidence, so that we may receive mercy and find grace to help us in our time of need."

Me: "Lord, what do You want me to know today?"

God: "Fear not what lies ahead for you, for I am going before you to prepare the way. I have given you no reason to fear anything, but every reason to trust in Me, for I love you with an everlasting love. You are secure with Me. I will show you how much I love you as we walk your life's journey together."

Is. 41:13 (NIV) ~ "For I am the Lord your God who takes hold of your right hand and says to you, Do not fear; I will help you."

Me: "Lord, what do You want me to know today?"

God: "See the way all creation in nature worships My Holy Name; you are to do the same. As the mountain streams babble and flow to where I direct them, so are you to let words of praise flow from your mouth as you go in the direction I lead you. Do not stop or take a detour—you will become stagnant, a stench in My nostrils. Instead, walk in the way everlasting, close by My side, and I will teach you and refresh your spirit like nothing on earth can do."

Is. 55:12 (NIV) ~ "You will go out in joy and be led forth in peace; the mountains and hills will burst into song before you, and all the trees of the field will clap their hands"

Me: "Lord, what do You want me to know today?"

God: "After I send rains on the earth, the budding plants bloom and the grass grows. In the same way, when I refresh you with the outpouring of My Holy Spirit upon your life, you also will grow and bloom, giving off a beautiful fragrance that will bless others as you love them with My eternal love. Be the fragrance that draws others to Me."

Is. 55:10-11 (NIV) ~ "As the rain and the snow come down from heaven, and do not return to it without watering the earth and making it bud and flourish, so that it yields seed for the sower and bread for the eater, so is my word that goes out from my mouth: It will not return to me empty, but will accomplish what I desire and achieve the purpose for which I sent it."

Me: "Lord, what do You want me to know today?"

God: "As soon as I give you an answer to that which you've prayed about, there will be no reason for you to doubt the direction I'm taking you. In the meantime, lean on Me and trust Me to handle it. I know what you need and when you'll need to know more about whatever concerns you.

"This journey you're on is much more amazing than you realize. Take it one step at a time, and don't look back. Give Me your hand and your heart daily—I have wonderful things to show you and teach you. There will be so much to discover as I lead you on the adventures I've created for you and Me to take together."

Ps. 34:4 (NIV) ~ "I sought the Lord, and he answered me; he delivered me from all my fears."

Me: "Lord, what do You want me to know today?"

God: "Stay the course. I am with you all the way. I will deflect the enemy's arrows so you can continue to move forward with Me along the path meant for you to take. This journey isn't easy, but I will teach you so many valuable lessons to treasure in your heart so that you may share with others who need to hear about My goodness in your life.

"Not all have the hope you've found in Me. Share your reason for hope with everyone you can. Be a light to those in darkness in your area of influence."

Matt. 5:16 (NIV) ~ "In the same way, let your light shine before others, that they may see your good deeds and glorify your Father in heaven."

Me: "Lord, what do You want me to know today?"

God: "Be sure in your heart of what you believe, for the enemy will test your convictions again and again. Do not waver in your faith walk, for many are watching you and learning about your love and faithfulness toward Me by the way you conduct yourself in your everyday pattern of living.

"Make your life a truthful testimony of My grace poured out for you at Calvary. Let there be no room for others to doubt your steadfastness in carrying out My kingdom work, right where I've put you, at any given time."

1 Cor. 15:58 (NIV) ~ "Therefore, my dear brothers and sisters, stand firm. Let nothing move you. Always give yourselves fully to the work of the Lord, because you know that your labor in the Lord is not in vain."

June 17

Me: "Lord, what do You want me to know today?"

God: "Search your motives before you come to Me in prayer. Are you asking that My will be done in your particular situation, or are you asking that I fulfill your own will for the way things will turn out? You must trust Me in all things even when you feel there is only one possible answer or solution to your problem. I created the world and everything in it; I can handle anything you are facing. My thoughts are not your thoughts.—you don't need to try to figure everything out.

"Let Me be the Author of your story. Your role is to live out the adventures I've created for you, right where I've placed you and with the people I've chosen who will take this journey with you."

James 4:3 (NIV) ~ "When you ask, you do not receive, because you ask with wrong motives, that you may spend what you get on your pleasures."

Me: "Lord, what do You want me to know today?"

God: "As surely as the sun rises in the east and sets in the west, I have given you a purpose on this earth. You are to share My Good News with others, using the gifts and talents I've given you. No one else has the same unique abilities and purpose that I've given you to use and carry out in your lifetime.

"When your life is lived in a way that reflects my love for you, the shine you'll give off will lead others to seek Me, also. Never be afraid to shine, for you may be the only light in someone else's darkest hour. Walk closely with Me and obey My nudging. I will handle the rest."

Rom. 13:12 (NIV) ~ "The night is nearly over; the day is almost here. So let us put aside the deeds of darkness and put on the armor of light."

Me: "Lord, what do You want me to know today?"

God: "I have given you My promise, through My Holy Word, that I will be with you always. Do not be troubled when you can't see the way ahead—I am leading you through every uncertainty that threatens to cause you to stumble. I will not let go of your hand. You are My beloved child."

Ps. 1:6 (NIV) ~ "For the Lord watches over the way of the righteous, but the way of the wicked leads to destruction."

Me: "Lord, what do You want me to know today?"

God: "There will be no purpose in your life that will go unfulfilled, as long as you follow My commands and seek Me with all of your heart. I will make known to you those things that are crucial pieces for the completion of My will in your life, as you petition Me for wisdom and discernment in every area that concerns you.

"Never lose faith in My ability to orchestrate, with beautiful results, the everyday events in your life. I delight in turning ordinary expectations into spectacular leaps of faith when My children learn to recognize My hand at work in situations they normally wouldn't think twice about."

Jer. 32:18-19 (NIV) ~ "...Great and mighty God, whose name is the Lord Almighty, great are your purposes and mighty are your deeds. Your eyes are open to the ways of all mankind; you reward each person according to their conduct and as their deeds deserve."

Me: "Lord, what do You want me to know today?"

God: "Over the course of your lifetime, I have been working out the details of My purpose for you. I have spared you from numerous calamities that didn't align with the plan I am unfolding day by day, that encompasses every aspect of your reason for being alive. I am completing a good work in you.

"Your job is to trust Me and commit every day into My hands for safekeeping, and then you are to live out the life I give you, and share My love with all those you come into contact with."

Ex. 15:11 (NIV) ~ "Who among the gods is like you, Lord? Who is like you—majestic in holiness, awesome in glory, working wonders?"

Me: "Lord, what do You want me to know today?"

God: "From the beginning of time, there has been a logical reason for the existence of everything I've created, including yourself. I planned perfectly the way every facet of your life would be integrated with the lives of those people I've written into your story for your time on earth.

"When you search for Me like a hidden jewel, I will reveal to you things too wondrous for you to comprehend otherwise. You will realize how deeply intertwined your personal choices and My will for you have been throughout your lifetime. And you will discover that what I've prepared for you to experience when you lean fully on Me will give you an insight into how much I love you, and an unsurpassable joy that is found only in My presence."

Ps. 40:5 (NIV) ~ "Many, Lord my God, are the wonders you have done, the things you planned for us. None can compare with you; were I to speak and tell of your deeds, they would be too many to declare."

Me: "Lord, what do You want me to know today?"

God: "Give ear to My Word and seek My counsel daily, for I have so much to tell you, to teach you, and to show you through the reading and application of what you'll learn from Me when you make this a priority in your schedule.

"There is nothing more important for the growth of your heart, mind, and soul than what awaits you when you feast upon My Holy Word and digest every truth found within. As you do so, My love for you will become more evident and familiar in such a way that you will not doubt My ability to lead you in the direction you should go, which will coincide with the greatest plans you've made for yourself."

Ps. 32:8 (NIV) ~ "I will instruct you and teach you in the way you should go; I will counsel you with my loving eye on you."

Me: "Lord, what do You want me to know today?"

God: "Wake up to what you know I require of you. Do not close your heart to Me when I direct you to do the hard things, for I am refining you because I love you.

"I am working out My perfect plan for you. I need your cooperation. Talk to Me. Spend time with Me. Ask Me to reveal to you My plans for you. I will show you what you were created to accomplish on this earth, and I will help you complete every task I give you."

Ps. 25:14-15 (NIV) ~ "The Lord confides in those who fear him; he makes his covenant known to them. My eyes are ever on the Lord, for only he will release my feet from the snare."

Me: "Lord, what do You want me to know today?"

God: "The areas where I am pruning your heart will be painful for a time afterward, but then new growth will occur, and you will feel Me at work giving you a fresh new outlook on your situation. Trust Me to help you flourish in the ways I created you to.

"There is so much I still intend for you to accomplish during your time on earth. Walk with Me, and let Me show you the greatest joys I've created just for you. The rest of your life can, and will, be the best of your life."

Ps. 111:7 (NIV) ~ "The works of his hands are faithful and just; all his precepts are trustworthy."

Me: "Lord, what do You want me to know today?"

God: "There are some things you will never get to know during your lifetime on earth. You don't need to figure everything out; that's where faith comes in—faith in your Heavenly Father's ability to work all things out for good where you are concerned. Leave the hard things to Me—I can handle them. Lean on Me for strength, and keep putting one foot in front of the other. I will lead you in the direction you should go.

"As we move forward together, you simply need to notice and take advantage of those opportunities I'll give you to use your gifts and talents in a way that will point others to the saving grace of My Son, Jesus Christ. In doing so, you will come to know the joy of fulfilling your God-given purpose in such a way that it is incomparable to anything else you'll experience on earth. Don't miss out on all I have in store for you."

Ps. 117:2 (NIV) ~ "For great is his love toward us, and the faithfulness of the Lord endures forever. Praise the Lord."

Me: "Lord, what do You want me to know today?"

God: "When the winds of change buffet you in ways you're unprepared for, remember that I have already gone ahead of you to align the course you're on with My perfect plans for you. Don't hesitate to call on My Name when the first pangs of uncertainty arise in your heart. I will always be there to walk you through whatever situation you find yourself in."

Ps. 5:3 (NIV) ~ "In the morning, Lord, you hear my voice; in the morning I lay my requests before you and wait expectantly."

Me: "Lord, what do You want me to know today?"

God: "Be careful to obey what I've told you to do, and follow My leading diligently; then I will show you what I want you to know about My character, and how I am developing your character to be more like My own.

"You become like those you spend time with. Spend time with Me on a regular basis, and let the essence of My Spirit breathe new life into you continuously. You, in turn, will become like a refreshing rain in the lives of those around you that are still dry like parched ground. As you receive from Me, so shall you pour out for the benefit of others, that My love may reach all people."

Ps. 37:18 (NIV) ~ "The blameless spend their days under the Lord's care, and their inheritance will endure forever."

Me: "Lord, what do You want me to know today?"

God: "Whatever is foremost on your mind is exactly what I want you to give over to Me. Do not hang onto something you can't control. Offer it to Me through prayer and surrender. I will give you the strength to endure your time of waiting, while I construct the details of your future according to My blueprint for your life.

"You will see how much I love you, even if things turn out differently than you hoped. I am always for you, never against you—believe it."

Ps. 86:4 (NIV) ~ "Bring joy to your servant, Lord, for I put my trust in you."

Me: "Lord, what do You want me to know today?"

God: "How long will it take for My people to realize the enormity of their sins and fall on their knees before Me in repentance? The eternity of every lost soul is at stake.

"Repentance begins in the heart. Don't look to others to be the leaders of a spiritual revival. Instead, let it begin with you. Repent of your sins daily. Ask Me to heal your family, your city, your country. I will hear you and will answer."

Matt. 13:15 (NIV) ~ "For this people's heart has become calloused; they hardly hear with their ears, and they have closed their eyes. Otherwise they might see with their eyes, hear with their ears, understand with their hearts and turn, and I would heal them."

July 1

Me: "Lord, what do You want me to know today?"

God: "There are some who will mock your allegiance to Me. They have not yet met Me, as you have. Pray for them, love them, be the reason they smile today. Go out of your way and do the uncomfortable things when I nudge you to do so. There will be a good reason for everything I ask you to do; just trust Me and obey when I call.

"The rewards reaped for My kingdom work on earth will be greater than you can imagine. Don't miss out on any opportunity I give you. Keep your eyes and ears open, and I will direct your paths."

John 16:3 (NIV) ~ "They will do such things because they have not known the Father or me."

Me: "Lord, what do You want me to know today?"

God: "Someone needs the gifts you have to offer. Do not use what I've given you to benefit only yourself. Freely give of your time and talents to encourage others for the glory of My Name. You will be blessed in doing so, and others will respond to My love as it pours from your heart. You are My ambassador."

Rom. 12:6-8 (NIV) ~ "We have different gifts, according to the grace given to each of us. If your gift is prophesying, then prophesy in accordance with your faith; if it is serving, then serve; if it is teaching, then teach; if it is to encourage, then give encouragement; if it is giving, then give generously; if it is to lead, do it diligently; if it is to show mercy, do it cheerfully."

Me: "Lord, what do You want me to know today?"

God: "Nothing you do will go unnoticed by Me, so let your actions reflect to the world a heart moved by My Spirit and not one that is callous to My leading, for you are My light to the lost in your immediate circle of influence.

"Be willing to shine brightly so those with dulled eyes may take notice and turn to Me before it is too late. Your sacrifice for My lost sheep will garner eternal treasures more valuable than anything the earth can offer."

1 John 3:18 (NIV) ~ "Dear children, let us not love with words or speech but with actions and in truth."

Me: "Lord, what do You want me to know today?"

God: "Go through your day with the utmost confidence in My abiding love for you. I have gone ahead of you to prepare your way. When you feel like giving up, give it all over to Me instead. I can handle your burdens, and I will turn your mourning into dancing as you learn to trust My perfect will for your life. There will be nothing you can't face in My strength."

Is. 26:3 (NIV) ~ "You will keep in perfect peace those whose minds are steadfast, because they trust in you."

Me: "Lord, what do You want me to know today?"

God: "Let there be no hesitation on your part when I make known to you My will for you at any given time. Obey Me without question, for I will always guide you in the direction you should go.

"When you falter in your faith in My timing, I will give you a reason for hope, that your trust in Me will remain steadfast. Always be alert to what I am teaching you through My Word, through your circumstances, and through interactions with others who cross your path. Your discoveries and revelations will be many when you are actively looking for Me at work in your life on a daily basis. I will show you things you would never see without a watchful eye."

Eph. 1:17-18 (NIV) ~ "I keep asking that the God of our Lord Jesus Christ, the glorious Father, may give you the Spirit of wisdom and revelation, so that you may know him better. I pray that the eyes of your heart may be enlightened in order that you may know the hope to which he has called you, the riches of his glorious inheritance in his holy people,"

Me: "Lord, what do You want me to know today?"

God: "I have given you more blessings in your day than you can count, if you will but look around and take notice. Each of these blessings is a sign of My love for you. What you do with them, for yourself and others, shows Me how you feel about My provision for you. A thankful heart is one of the best ways to bless and honor your Heavenly Father."

1 Chron. 16:34 (NIV) ~ "Give thanks to the Lord, for he is good; his love endures forever."

Me: "Lord, what do You want me to know today?"

God: "All those who come to Me with their burdens find rest for their soul, and peace of mind, as I lift the heaviness from their shoulders. You have experienced this, time after time. Be diligent in sharing My love with others, that they may also come to know Me and receive the gift of grace I have waiting for them. Gifts are meant to be shared, and no burden needs to be carried alone.

"When you come alongside those with heavy hearts, in love and sincerity, the walls of fear and distrust will come down, and seeds of hope and faith may be planted there. Never give up on anyone. Keep praying and making yourself available to them as needs arise. You will be blessed by what I will do through your compassionate gestures toward those I put on your heart."

2 Cor. 1:3-4 (NIV) ~ "Praise be to the God and Father of our Lord Jesus Christ, the Father of compassion and the God of all comfort, who comforts us in all our troubles, so that we can comfort those in any trouble with the comfort we ourselves receive from God."

Me: "Lord, what do You want me to know today?"

God: "The choices you make today will reflect your relationship with Me, so be sure to think before you act, and pray for wisdom and discernment to be able to hear and obey the still small voice of My Holy Spirit speaking into your life. Then you will be able to bless others as you willingly submit to My leading, for they will see the grace of God being poured out through you and know that they are loved."

Prov. 8:10 (NIV) ~ "Choose my instruction instead of silver, knowledge rather than choice gold,"

Me: "Lord, what do You want me to know today?"

God: "I have given you a purpose to carry out, which will only require your obedience, not necessarily your understanding—yet. I will give you the strength needed to complete the task at hand. Follow My nudging; you will know when you've been nudged—don't ignore it.

"Step out in faith, even when you're not sure which direction to go. I will lead you to where you are meant to be, and I will develop in you a heart of confidence, that you may move forward with a renewed purpose, and in so doing, fulfill My perfect will for you."

Ps. 128:1 (NIV) ~ "Blessed are all who fear the Lord, who walk in obedience to him."

Me: "Lord, what do You want me to know today?"

God: "There will come a time when you will recognize My holiness as being the most important aspect of your life on earth. Not only that, but the more closely you walk with Me each day, the more of My glory I will reveal to you.

"There is nothing on earth that can compare to what I will show you when you come to Me in humbleness of heart and acknowledge your need for Me in every area of your life. I will restore what the locusts have eaten. I will give you My blessing in such a way that you can't yet even imagine. Never underestimate the great plans I have for your life."

1 Chron. 29:11 (NIV) ~ "Yours, Lord, is the greatness and the power and the glory and the majesty and the splendor, for everything in heaven and earth is yours. Yours, Lord, is the kingdom; you are exalted as head over all."

Me: "Lord, what do You want me to know today?"

God: "Be sure of this: I am doing something in your life that will forever change the way you think about Me. I am opening your eyes to see more profoundly how I am at work in your life on a constant basis. I am showing you the areas of your life that need to be surrendered to Me.

"As you relinquish to Me those things you hold so tightly to, that are detrimental to your spiritual growth, I will in return empower you to flourish as you come to understand the full capacity of the gifts and talents I've created you with and the great joy you will discover in using them for My glory."

Heb. 13:21 (NIV) ~ "...equip you with everything good for doing his will, and may he work in us what is pleasing to him, through Jesus Christ, to whom be glory for ever and ever. Amen."

Me: "Lord, what do You want me to know today?"

God: "Let your life be spent in willingness to follow My leading, oblivious to the lures of the world around you. You were made for a greater purpose than that of following the crowd. Be a light in this dark world. Be courageous in the areas of eternal significance that I will reveal to you. Be led by the Holy Spirit, and not by your flesh.

"Let Me show you great and wonderful things that can only be seen by a heart fully surrendered to My leading. You were given this life for a purpose—let Me show you My perspective, that your joy may be full."

Rom. 15:13 (NIV) ~ "May the God of hope fill you with all joy and peace as you trust in him, so that you may overflow with hope by the power of the Holy Spirit."

Me: "Lord, what do You want me to know today?"

God: "Rest in Me, and let Me carry your burdens today. I will finish in your life the good work I started, and your requirement will be to remain faithful to My calling and My leading. Every day you have a choice to listen to and obey Me or to ignore Me and go your own way. One choice will lead to life, fulfillment, and joy, while the other will take you in the direction of death and destruction even as you still live on this earth.

"Don't waste a single day dabbling in folly, but rather, be purposeful in carrying out My will for you, that others may see and know that I love them. It is by your faithful service to Me that some will come to saving faith in Christ Jesus, even when you are not aware of it."

Prov. 2:8 (NIV) ~ "for he guards the course of the just and protects the way of his faithful ones."

Me: "Lord, what do You want me to know today?"

God: "I know your heart. I know every wound, every scar left behind when the words or actions of others pierced you like arrows. I bore your pain at Calvary. Just as I have forgiven your every sin, you are to do likewise toward those who have sinned against you. Do not harbor anger in your heart. Instead, release to Me your burdens, and receive My peace in return.

"Consider yourself worthy, as My child, to be valued and treasured, for you are uniquely created and gifted like no one else. Look to Me for all the encouragement you need, for no one can love you more than your Heavenly Father."

2 Thess. 2:16-17 (NIV) ~ "May our Lord Jesus Christ himself and God our Father, who loved us and by his grace gave us eternal encouragement and good hope, encourage your hearts and strengthen you in every good deed and word."

Me: "Lord, what do You want me to know today?"

God: "When I do something recognizable in your life that points to My glory and My intervention on your behalf, do not hesitate to share this revelation with others as a witness to My Divine love for My children.

"Use every opportunity you are given to reflect the hope you have in Christ Jesus in a tangible way, that others may come to see Me in a new light and realize that I am very reachable at all times, just a prayer away and ready to respond to a heartfelt cry with open arms at a moment's notice. Ask My Holy Spirit to give you the words to say, and be a trusting vessel, willing to be used by Him this way. Your faith will lead others in the right direction."

Col. 4:6 (NIV) ~ "Let your conversation be always full of grace, seasoned with salt, so that you may know how to answer everyone."

Me: "Lord, what do You want me to know today?"

God: "Continue to give Me the burdens you bear. Fervently pray in all circumstances, for there is unlimited power within your reach when you pray in the Name of Jesus. Don't forsake this resource, this tool I've given you, which brings you before My throne immediately. No matter where you're at or what your circumstances are, call out to Me anytime and believe that your prayers are being heard. I have an answer for every prayer. Trust Me to stand in the gap at the right time—My perfect timing never fails.

"When you don't know what to say in prayer, ask My Holy Spirit to intercede on your behalf. I will hear Him and answer. Cover your loved ones in prayer. Cover your enemies in prayer. Leave no stone unturned as you pray for others, for your greatest gift to them is petitioning the Father to work on their behalf. Watch for answers to your prayers. Write them down. Share them with others, that they may be encouraged by, and reminded of, My faithfulness."

Ps. 66:20 (NIV) ~ "Praise be to God, who has not rejected my prayer or withheld his love from me!"

Me: "Lord, what do You want me to know today?"

God: "When the wind blows, it carries with it seeds of change. Wherever these seeds fall, sprout, and blossom, there will be new life and new growth.

"I am scattering seeds of change in your life also, that you may bloom, grow, and flourish in new areas. Don't be afraid to experience all that I have for you to learn and discover in the days ahead. I will walk beside you on this amazing journey, and you will find out how strong and resilient I created you to be."

Josh. 1:9 (NIV) ~ "Have I not commanded you? Be strong and courageous. Do not be afraid; do not be discouraged, for the Lord your God will be with you wherever you go."

Me: "Lord, what do You want me to know today?"

God: "There is rarely a reason for anger in your life other than righteous anger, which erupts when you know someone is openly and defiantly shaking their fist at Me in such a way that brings harm to themselves or others. In many circumstances, love will trump anger and cause walls to crumble. If you recall times when someone reacted to you in love, rather than anger, you will remember how encouraged and uplifted you felt by that simple act toward you on their part. When you could've been dragged down by hurtful words or actions, an act of loving-kindness instead brightened your outlook.

"Practice showing grace toward others even in the smallest interactions you encounter. Loving words seasoned with grace will be powerful diffusers in tense situations. Decide ahead of time how you want to react when anger threatens your disposition, and you will have time to practice your response accordingly."

Eph. 4:26 (NIV) ~ "'In your anger do not sin': Do not let the sun go down while you are still angry,"

Me: "Lord, what do You want me to know today?"

God: "When you sense Me nudging you to let go of habits that get in the way of the work I'm doing in your life, listen and obey Me. Your joy will come from openly acknowledging My will for you and putting that ahead of your own will for the way things turn out in your life.

"Serve Me with a happy and willing heart in all you do, and trust Me to fulfill your dreams in My perfect timing. Nothing can compare to the blessings that await you when everything you do is done with the intent of bringing Me honor and glory."

Deut. 13:4 (NIV) ~ "It is the Lord your God you must follow, and him you must revere. Keep his commands and obey him; serve him and hold fast to him."

Me: "Lord, what do You want me to know today?"

God: "Secure your footing by standing on My Word. Speak My promises out loud, and often, when you feel the enemy closing in on you. The power of Jesus' Name, when spoken by My children in prayer, is unmatchable— able to conquer any and every stronghold in your life.

"Use these tools often, for they will reinforce your faith in Me as you see the results of My love for you being trans- formed into tangible answers to your prayers, which will come at the right times, according to My perfect plan for you."

Prov. 18:10 (NIV) ~ "The name of the Lord is a fortified tower; the righteous run to it and are safe."

Me: "Lord, what do You want me to know today?"

God: "Because I've given you a life and a legacy to live out on this earth, there is no time for frivolous pursuits. Center your efforts on what I've given you to complete for My kingdom purpose so that it will not be left undone and remain fruitless when your time on earth is finished.

"When you see how I will bless your efforts, you will gain the courage to continue on with all that I have yet to entrust you with. I will help you finish well as you keep your eyes and heart transfixed on Me."

Phil. 3:12-14 (NIV) ~ "Not that I have already obtained all this, or have already arrived at my goal, but I press on to take hold of that for which Christ Jesus took hold of me. Brothers and sisters, I do not consider myself yet to have taken hold of it. But one thing I do: Forgetting what is behind and straining toward what is ahead, I press on toward the goal to win the prize for which God has called me heavenward in Christ Jesus."

Me: "Lord, what do You want me to know today?"

God: "Let there be no person, no object, no attitude, no dream of yours that comes between you and Me as a form of idol worship. You must worship Me alone. I am the Giver of gifts. I will bless your relationships as you lay them at My feet and acknowledge My sovereignty regarding everyone you associate with. I will give you all that you need, that you may be content as you trust Me to direct you in your financial dealings. Your attitude should be one of joy and thanksgiving as you reflect on all the ways I am and have been directly involved in your everyday pursuits and struggles.

"You never have to walk this road alone. I am with you, and I have gone before you to prepare the way that I am taking you because I love you, and I know what it will take to mesh My plans with your dreams in order that My purpose for your life will be fully carried out. Do you trust Me? I will continue to show you My faithfulness as you relinquish everything into My hands daily, as an offering to the One you choose to love and serve first and foremost."

Ps. 31:14 (NIV) ~ "But I trust in you, Lord; I say, 'You are my God.'"

Me: "Lord, what do You want me to know today?"

God: "When you speak to others, let your words be encouraging and uplifting. Make the extra effort to shine My light wherever you go, no matter the discomfort you feel at the time. Ask Me to give you guidance, and then trust Me to help you carry out My will in your interactions with others.

"The eternal benefits of your obedience will always out-weigh the temporary inconvenience you may feel when I ask you to step out of your comfort zone and extend grace to another person I cross your path with."

Rom. 15:5-6 (NIV) ~ "May the God who gives endurance and encouragement give you the same attitude of mind toward each other that Christ Jesus had, so that with one mind and one voice you may glorify the God and Father of our Lord Jesus Christ."

Me: "Lord, what do You want me to know today?"

God: "When you depend on Me in a way that points to My deity being greater than your humanness, you are acknowledging Me as the source of all you truly need on a minute-by-minute/day-by-day basis.

"When you point others toward My glory, you will reflect the radiance of Christ, and others will be drawn to Me through your willingness to be a light."

John 3:30 (NIV) ~ "He must become greater; I must become less."

Me: "Lord, what do You want me to know today?"

God: "There is no one who loves you more than I do. When I give you a promise through My Word, I will always keep it.

"Do not be deceived by the one who seeks to destroy your allegiance to Me. He will twist My truths and use them to his advantage as he attempts to manipulate your heart. Stand firm on the foundation I laid for you at Calvary through the death and resurrection of My Son, Jesus Christ. You will be tested time and again as you live out your faith for My Name's sake. Darkness will not overtake the one who uses My Word as a weapon of defense in times of spiritual warfare. Never fear anything that threatens to undo you; instead, see it for what it is— a snare of the enemy. Then, pray about it in the powerful Name of Jesus, and victory will be yours."

Ps. 60:12 (NIV) ~ "With God we will gain the victory, and he will trample down our enemies."

Me: "Lord, what do You want me to know today?"

God: "Scale your activities to fit within the parameters I've drawn for you so that you have time to spend with the One Who breathed life into you and gave you a hope and a future. As you open your heart to Me through prayer and the reading of My Holy Word, I will reveal My heart to you, also, and you will know the depth of My love for you in a way that no human can explain."

Ps. 89:15 (NIV) ~ "Blessed are those who have learned to acclaim you, who walk in the light of your presence, Lord."

Me: "Lord, what do You want me to know today?"

God: "When I have something to tell you, do not turn your ear away; rather, lean in closer and listen fervently to My words of instruction to you. The benefits of doing so will far outweigh any other distraction that competes for your attention. What I tell you will always be applicable to your current heart condition. Receive My words to you as an outpouring of My love toward you, and ask Me for wisdom when you need a deeper understanding of what I'm telling you.

"There is no situation you will face alone when you're walking closely with Me. You will learn to recognize My voice more easily when you make it a habit to spend time with Me regularly."

John 10:27 (NIV) ~ "My sheep listen to my voice; I know them, and they follow me."

Me: "Lord, what do You want me to know today?"

God: "Seeing is believing. When you keep your eyes open, watching for the things I am doing in your life, you will see and understand that there is something much greater going on than mere circumstance. I have a Divine purpose for everything you experience, with a righteous intention of reminding you how much I love you.

"When you willingly submit your moments and your days into My hands, I will satisfy your longings in a way you could never do on your own. I know what you need, and when you need it, in order that you may fulfill the purpose I've given you on this earth—the purpose that will enable you to know your greatest moments of joy while serving your King and loving the people I've given you to take this journey with."

Ps. 59:9 (NIV) ~ "You are my strength, I watch for you; you, God, are my fortress,"

Me: "Lord, what do You want me to know today?"

God: "I have shown you My glory in many ways over the course of your lifetime. I continue to show you My glory every day. If you're watching for it, you will see it. Open your eyes to the things I am doing in your life. Acknowledge them. Write them down. Share them with others, that they may hear and believe that I am God, and may know that I love My children and desire to be actively involved in the lives of those who call Me Lord and Savior.

"When you take time in your day to listen for My voice, you will hear Me. Be still before Me and receive what I have for you; then your heart will be filled with the knowledge of the glory of the Lord, and you shall go forth in peace, with My blessing."

Ps. 66:5 (NIV) ~ "Come and see what God has done, his awesome deeds for mankind!"

Me: "Lord, what do You want me to know today?"

God: "Go forward in the areas I've already prepared you for. Do all that you are able to do with the talents and resources I've blessed you with so far. I will guide you as you go, and I will open the right doors for you when you come to them.

"Trust Me to take you through the unknown valleys that lie ahead, and to get you to where you need to be for the fulfillment of My purpose in your days to come. As you walk with Me, you will find that I have many blessings in store for you. Never doubt how much I love you."

Ps. 48:14 (NIV) ~ "For this God is our God for ever and ever; he will be our guide even to the end."

Me: "Lord, what do You want me to know today?"

God: "When it seems you can't see the way ahead, that is when I am right in front of you, leading the way. I will always make a sure path for you in the direction you should go. Call out to Me whenever you feel like you're losing your footing—I will get you back on track and show you My blessings along the way to keep you encouraged."

Ps. 23:3 (NIV) ~ "he refreshes my soul. He guides me along the right paths for his name's sake."

Me: "Lord, what do You want me to know today?"

God: "From the realms of Heaven, I hear every word you say to Me, I hear every thought you think, and I care about all that concerns you. My will for you is that you come to Me daily and lay all your burdens at My feet. Let Me fill you with My peace as you let go of the things you can't control. There is no reason for you to doubt what I am doing through your present circumstances.

"I have shown you continuously how much I love you, and I will not fail to work out My perfect plan in your life. Enjoy the blessings of this day, and look for ways to bless others, also. Even a small act of kindness can be like a balm for a hurting soul."

Is. 26:12 (NIV) ~ "Lord, you establish peace for us; all that we have accomplished you have done for us."

Me: "Lord, what do You want me to know today?"

God: "A sincere heart is what I ask of you—that you give Me your whole self, not just pieces of your heart. Come to Me in worship and humbleness with a heart that is laid bare before Me. I will listen to your pain and weep with you. I will uphold you with My mighty right hand.

"You will feel My love and My strength as I carry out My transformation work within you for the glory of My Holy Name. I will open your spiritual eyes, that you may see and recognize My hand at work in your life. In even the smallest details of your day I will show you My glory."

Ps. 25:8-10 (NIV) ~ "Good and upright is the Lord; therefore he instructs sinners in his ways. He guides the humble in what is right and teaches them his way. All the ways of the Lord are loving and faithful toward those who keep the demands of his covenant."

Me: "Lord, what do You want me to know today?"

God: "My arms are a haven for you; come rest in My loving embrace often. I will renew you and restore you that you may go forth in confidence, prepared to face anything I ask you to do, with the knowledge that I will enable you and equip you as needed.

"There will be nothing too difficult to overcome when you continually look to Me as the source of your strength. I will move mountains for you just to show you how much I love you."

1 Pet. 5:10 (NIV) ~ "And the God of all grace, who called you to his eternal glory in Christ, after you have suffered a little while, will himself restore you and make you strong, firm and steadfast."

Me: "Lord, what do You want me to know today?"

God: "Where there is light, there is life. You are to be the light for those in darkness. Do not let your compassion for others become dull. When you see someone in need, act upon it immediately. If you are unable to help, find someone who can.

"I have given you My Holy Spirit to lead you and guide your thoughts and actions. Listen to the Voice of Truth and live by giving of yourself through a heart of sacrifice, as I have given to you through the sacrifice of My Son, Jesus Christ. There will always be someone in need. Pay attention and respond when you feel My nudge. Let Me teach you how to give unsparingly from the wealth of My Kingdom, which flows through your heart."

Luke 11:36 (NIV) ~ "Therefore, if your whole body is full of light, and no part of it dark, it will be just as full of light as when a lamp shines its light on you."

Me: "Lord, what do You want me to know today?"

God: "Reach for My hand on a daily basis. I will guide you through the rocky places that lie ahead. Keep your eyes fixed on Me, and I will lead you in the direction you should go. When you hear My voice, answer Me in obedience without hesitation. There are good reasons for everything I allow you to experience. I am growing your character and molding your heart, that you may become more like Me and less like the world.

"The value I place on you is priceless—so treasured are you in My sight. I will cover you with My love all the days of your life, and you will know the riches of the Kingdom of Heaven even as you still walk on the earth."

Ps. 73:23 (NIV) ~ "Yet I am always with you; you hold me by my right hand."

Me: "Lord, what do You want me to know today?"

God: "There will be nothing too great for you to accomplish when you walk steadfastly with Me. If you go your own way, however, the hindrances will be many, and destructive at that—sin works that way. You will not find peace apart from Me. Commit your ways to My safe-keeping, and I will not lead you astray.

"Encourage one another in the way you should go, always speaking the truth in love, seasoned with grace. Pray without ceasing, and believe that I am always at work on your behalf for the purpose of My will being made complete in your life."

Ps. 51:10 (NIV) ~ "Create in me a pure heart, O God, and renew a steadfast spirit within me."

Me: "Lord, what do You want me to know today?"

God: "There is a time to be still and a time to act. Don't count on your own ability to know what to do at any given time. Ask Me to give you sure guidance in any and every circumstance—this is not a show of weakness on your part, but rather, an indicator that you know where your true strength comes from and Who deserves the glory for this."

Ps. 59:17 (NIV) ~ "You are my strength, I sing praise to you; you, God, are my fortress, my God on whom I can rely."

August 8

Me: "Lord, what do You want me to know today?"

God: "Just as a baker adds yeast to the dough to make the bread rise, so do I work My Words of Truth into the soft and fertile areas of your heart so that you may continue to be fed by the Bread of Life on a daily basis.

"It's up to you to read My Word, respond to the nudging of the Holy Spirit, and act upon what I'm teaching you in order to share with others that which feeds and nourishes your soul. Many are spiritually hungry and searching for a way to feed this hunger with something the world has to offer. Be My ambassador—lead them to My table, that they may be truly satisfied."

John 6:35 (NIV) ~ "Then Jesus declared, "I am the bread of life. Whoever comes to me will never go hungry, and whoever believes in me will never be thirsty."

Me: "Lord, what do You want me to know today?"

God: "Wherever I send you to minister to others, be assured that I have gone there ahead of you to prepare hearts and minds to receive that which I will give you to share with them. Do not be afraid of what I will ask you to say or do—just go when I call you to do so.

"Lives will be changed through your obedience to Me. Hearts will be softened because of your sacrifices made for others for the glory of My Holy Name."

1 Pet. 3:14 (NIV) ~ "But even if you should suffer for what is right, you are blessed. 'Do not fear their threats; do not be frightened.'"

Me: "Lord, what do You want me to know today?"

God: "There is a reason for your restless heart—those things you hold onto so tightly are holding you back from receiving My best for you. Your interpretation of what's good for you is nowhere near the level of magnificence I intend to bestow upon you when you let Me have full reign in your life. The sooner you release your grip on the things you can't control (that are actually controlling you), the better you will be able to focus on what really matters and make true progress in the areas I've created you to excel in.

"Ask Me for wisdom and guidance each day, and follow the directions I give you through the nudging of My Holy Spirit. Be willing and ready to experience more than you could imagine in your wildest dreams. My love has no limits."

Is. 28:29 (NIV) ~ "All this also comes from the Lord Almighty, whose plan is wonderful, whose wisdom is magnificent."

Me: "Lord, what do You want me to know today?"

God: "Show Me your true heart of repentance; don't just speak the words—work on the changes you need to make in your life, which I've told you are necessary. There will be setbacks along the way, but don't be deterred by them; I am leading you forward with determination to see you become all I've created you to be.

"Don't listen to what others are telling you you need to be, but listen to My voice, through the Holy Spirit living in you. I know you better than anyone, and I will show you My best for you when you focus on Me as your number one source of strength and guidance on a daily basis. My great love for you will be evident to others who are watching you evolve into the beautiful masterpiece I've designed you to become for the glory of My Holy Name."

Is. 30:18 (NIV) ~ "Yet the Lord longs to be gracious to you; therefore he will rise up to show you compassion. For the Lord is a God of justice. Blessed are all who wait for him!"

Me: "Lord, what do You want me to know today?"

God: "Do not succumb to the temptations of the world, as so many do. Your treasure is to be stored up in heaven, through your willingness to be poured out for My kingdom purpose.

"Throw open the doors of your heart and be ready to receive those whom I send to you, who need to hear about the love of Jesus, that they may also receive the gift of eternal life as you have—the greatest treasure, bought and paid for by the redeeming blood of My one and only Son, Jesus Christ. Be My messenger of light and life, for you have been given a hope and a treasure that increases in value the more you share it with others."

Matt. 6:19-21 (NIV) ~ "Do not store up for yourselves treasures on earth, where moths and vermin destroy, and where thieves break in and steal. But store up for yourselves treasures in heaven, where moths and vermin do not destroy, and where thieves do not break in and steal. For where your treasure is, there your heart will be also."

Me: "Lord, what do You want me to know today?"

God: "Remember that I don't expect perfection from you, but only a heart that is moldable and willing to be challenged as I lead you in the way I want you to go. I will teach you what I want you to learn as you walk with Me on this journey of your lifetime.

"Shake off the fears and get moving. A world of wonder awaits you, which I have planned for you, specifically, to experience. Don't wait another moment. Put one foot in front of the other, and I will show you that nothing you fear can stop My perfect will for you from being carried out as you obediently submit to My leading."

Ps. 119:108 (NIV) ~ "Accept, Lord, the willing praise of my mouth, and teach me your laws."

Me: "Lord, what do You want me to know today?"

God: "Keep focusing on My purpose for your life. If you're not sure what it is, ask Me to show you. Ask Me every day to give you direction and wisdom. I will guide your steps in the way you should go—but first, you need to start moving forward.

"Attitude is a big key in your role of obedience to Me. Don't let your attitude stop you from coming with Me on a journey that will transform your heart and mind for all time. There will be no limit to what I can accomplish through your willing heart, open and poured out into the lives of others for the glory of My Holy Name."

Matt. 7:7-8 (NIV) ~ "Ask and it will be given to you; seek and you will find; knock and the door will be opened to you. For everyone who asks receives; the one who seeks finds; and to the one who knocks, the door will be opened."

Me: "Lord, what do You want me to know today?"

God: "Let Me calm your heart and mind as you rest in My presence. There will always be things to think about and things to do, but the moments you spend with Me will be where you find your true strength as I pour My life-giving truths into your heart when you are willing to receive them.

"Do not hesitate to talk to Me throughout your day, for I am always here for you. Tell Me everything. I want to hear your heartfelt cries in good times and bad. Trust Me with what matters most to you. The more you get to know Me, the more you will see My faithfulness in your life."

Ps. 34:17 (NIV) ~ "The righteous cry out, and the Lord hears them; he delivers them from all their troubles."

Me: "Lord, what do You want me to know today?"

God: "Find moments of rest in your day. Don't let every minute be packed with busyness. I gave you eyes so you can look around and see the beauty of the world I made for your pleasure and Mine.

"Take time to notice the needs of those people I cross your paths with. Unravel your priorities, and create something new and beautiful in the lives of those who don't share your joy. The best gifts are not things, but experiences shared with others."

1 Thess. 3:9 (NIV) ~ "How can we thank God enough for you in return for all the joy we have in the presence of our God because of you?"

Me: "Lord, what do You want me to know today?"

God: "When you share the burdens of others, you share My heart in a tangible way. Be willing to be the hands and feet of Christ whenever I nudge you to do so.

"Watch for every opportunity to bless someone out of the abundance I've given you. You've been on the receiving end of such grace, and I also give you opportunities to be the blessing for others. As long as your heart is willing, you will never lack the needed resources I will ask you to pour into the lives of others. I will always provide what you need at the right time."

Rom. 12:13 (NIV) ~ "Share with the Lord's people who are in need. Practice hospitality."

Me: "Lord, what do You want me to know today?"

God: "Where there are uncertainties in your life, you can be sure I am working things out in a way that will be beneficial to everyone involved. If you give Me the reins, I will steer you in the right direction. You never have to worry about losing your way when I am in control.

"Commit your every concern to Me, and I will walk you through the necessary resolution in a way that will affirm your faith in My ability to carry out My perfect will and delight your heart, at the same time."

Ps. 25:9 (NIV) ~ "He guides the humble in what is right and teaches them his way."

Me: "Lord, what do You want me to know today?"

God: "Be diligent and intentional in your walk with Me. Make sure your words match your actions, that no one may be led astray by the message you convey in the way you live your life. Exalt My Name in your conversations with others. Speak My truths aloud to yourself often, so you will become familiar enough with them to share them with others when I prompt you to do so.

"Your significance for My kingdom purpose will be much greater when you are equipped with the tools I've given you. A tool is only useful if it's used, and it takes practice to learn how to use a tool in the most effective way. My Holy Word is the instruction manual for your life. Read it and learn how to truly live; then, share freely with others what you've learned."

Ps. 40:10 (NIV) ~ "I do not hide your righteousness in my heart; I speak of your faithfulness and your saving help. I do not conceal your love and your faithfulness from the great assembly."

Me: "Lord, what do You want me to know today?"

God: "What seems impossible to you is merely another chance for Me to show you My glory, if you will be patient and wait as I work things out in a way that I know is best for you. Don't lose hope when you can't see what I am doing. Call on My Name whenever you feel alone, for I am right here with you always. I will be your strength when the enemy attacks. Ask Me to open your eyes, that you may see the blessings in your life and know the abundance of My love for you.

"Keep moving forward with what I give you daily to work on; then, you will be ready for the next big assignment when I hand it to you. Your life is never without purpose. Come to Me with a willing heart each day, and follow My leading; I will not let you forget your value as My child— priceless, forever loved, cherished, and adored."

Ps. 33:18 (NIV) ~ "But the eyes of the Lord are on those who fear him, on those whose hope is in his unfailing love,"

Me: "Lord, what do You want me to know today?"

God: "No one else on earth can carry out what I've given you to do with the gifts and talents I created you with. I can use other people to accomplish any task I've planned for you to do, but it still would not be the same way you would've done it, which would be uniquely your style and no one else's.

"Don't miss out on the chances I give you to leave this world a better place than it was when you entered it. Eagerly accept what I give you to do, and put your all into it. I will bless your efforts and multiply them in ways that will encourage others to follow your example of obedience to My calling in your life."

2 Cor. 8:11-12 (NIV) ~ "Now finish the work, so that your eager willingness to do it may be matched by your completion of it, according to your means. For if the willingness is there, the gift is acceptable according to what one has, not according to what one does not have."

Me: "Lord, what do You want me to know today?"

God: "Service to others is one way you show your love for Me. There is always someone in need of what you have to offer. Generosity comes in many forms. When you serve others with no expectations in return, something beautiful happens—hearts are awakened and stirred by this tangible expression of grace being freely poured out.

"I always know who is in need, what they need, and when they need it. Don't ignore My nudging if I ask you to reach out to someone, specifically, for you may be the very tool I will use to supply just what they need at a crucial time in their life, which may even be instrumental in leading them to understand and receive the gift of salvation. Never underestimate what I can accomplish through the willing obedience of a generous heart."

1 Pet. 4:10 (NIV) ~ "Each of you should use whatever gift you have received to serve others, as faithful stewards of God's grace in its various forms."

Me: "Lord, what do You want me to know today?"

God: "When I show you My glory in your everyday circumstances, I do it so that your faith in My provision for you will continue to grow and flourish. I am involved in the outcome of everything you go through—good and bad. There are always blessings in each situation. When you look for the blessings, you will see My glory. Your heart will be encouraged, and your faith will be strengthened. As you share with others the stories of these blessings in your life, they, in turn, will be encouraged to take note of how I am working in their lives, also."

Ps. 27:13 (NIV) ~ "I remain confident of this: I will see the goodness of the Lord in the land of the living."

Me: "Lord, what do You want me to know today?"

God: "When you focus on My will as you pray, rather than your own desires, I will make known to you that which will have a profound effect on the way you look at your life. You will no longer feel such a need to ask for things as you will a need to receive with open hands, in thankfulness, all that I want to give you. Trust Me in everything and receive what I know is best for you."

Eph. 4:1-3 (NIV) ~ "As a prisoner for the Lord, then, I urge you to live a life worthy of the calling you have received. Be completely humble and gentle; be patient, bearing with one another in love. Make every effort to keep the unity of the Spirit through the bond of peace."

Me: "Lord, what do You want me to know today?"

God: "Show Me your devotion to Me by the way you serve others who can't repay you. Let your motivation come from a heart of thanksgiving for all I've given you, that others may see and know My goodness also, as you simply obey what I give you to do.

"Share My love with others, every chance you get, that they may come to realize how special they are to Me and be given an opportunity to know Me like you do."

2 Cor. 9:12 (NIV) ~ "This service that you perform is not only supplying the needs of the Lord's people but is also overflowing in many expressions of thanks to God."

Me: "Lord, what do You want me to know today?"

God: "Search your heart to find those things you are holding onto that dim your view of Me and prevent you from becoming all I've created you to be. Lay these things at My feet and ask Me to remove them for good.

"Ask Me, also, to fill your empty places with more of Myself. Do not be afraid of transformation—what I am doing in your life will reveal to you how precious you are to Me. No one can steal from you what I have purposed for you to complete as you seek Me first above all else."

Ps. 4:3-5 (NIV) ~ "Know that the Lord has set apart his faithful servant for himself; the Lord hears when I call to him. Tremble and do not sin; when you are on your beds, search your hearts and be silent. Offer the sacrifices of the righteous and trust in the Lord."

Me: "Lord, what do You want me to know today?"

God: "Choose wisely how you will spend the time, gifts, and talents I've entrusted to you. Search your heart and uncover the motives that lead you in the direction you most often go. Are you content to wait on Me and follow My leading, or are you rushing ahead blindly, with the fear of being left behind while others attain their goals and enjoy the taste of success?"

Prov. 16:1-3 (NIV) ~ "People make plans in their hearts. But the Lord puts the correct answer on their tongues. Everything a person does might seem pure to them. But the Lord knows why they do what they do. Commit to the Lord everything you do. Then he will make your plans succeed."

Me: "Lord, what do You want me to know today?"

God: "Seize the moments I give you that can be spent in prayer. Make it a habit to come before My throne in prayer every time you feel a concern about someone or something.

"Thinking about someone is not the same as praying for them. When you petition Me in the powerful Name of Jesus, on behalf of yourself or someone else, I will set into motion the necessary components I've chosen to use in answering your prayer. There is no limit to what I will accomplish when you come before Me with a heart of humble sincerity, seeking My will in every area of need."

Col. 4:2 (NIV) ~ "Devote yourselves to prayer, being watchful and thankful."

Me: "Lord, what do You want me to know today?"

God: "There is none other like you on earth, which is just how I planned it. No one else delights Me in the same way you do. I gave you My best for you in the way I created you. Receive all I've given you, with thanksgiving, for I've supplied you with every gift you need to be able to blossom and flourish in a beautiful way.

"You were designed to be a reflection of My love for you, with every breath you take, with every move you make, using your gifts for My glory in a broken world. Because you are uniquely created, you need never worry about fitting in—just be yourself, and let Me decide who will benefit from what I've given you to carry out for My kingdom purpose."

Ps. 52:8 (NIV) ~ "But I am like an olive tree flourishing in the house of God; I trust in God's unfailing love for ever and ever."

Me: "Lord, what do You want me to know today?"

God: "Remember those times when I've allowed you to explore paths that ended up being detrimental to your well-being; I gave you freedom of choice, and you exercised it. Remember, also, those times when you chose to follow a path I led you on and the peace you felt in your heart as a result of your obedience to Me. In each instance, you had a choice to make. The results of your choices, however, were greatly different.

"You still get to make many choices every day, some of which affect more people than just yourself. Are you doing this in your own strength, drawing from your own limited wisdom and ability, or are you relying on My sovereignty to guide and direct you as you call on Me in prayer before you act?"

James 1:5 (NIV) ~ "If any of you lacks wisdom, you should ask God, who gives generously to all without finding fault, and it will be given to you."

Me: "Lord, what do You want me to know today?"

God: "Factors you can't control will always be a part of your life. How you react to them is reflective of how much you trust Me when you can't see the outcome.

"Let your faith become bigger than your doubts and fears as you allow Me to stretch you in areas you're not comfortable with. I know how resilient I've created you to be. Relax, and let Me turn your struggles into an adventure that will be yours and Mine together. You will grow in your ability to thrive when you acknowledge and proclaim your dependence on Me as your Best Friend, Provider, and Mentor in every area of your life, every day."

Ps. 62:6 (NIV) ~ "Truly he is my rock and my salvation; he is my fortress, I will not be shaken."

Me: "Lord, what do You want me to know today?"

God: "Be still before Me, and I will give you rest—not the kind of rest the world offers, but a deep, abiding peace that will fill your heart and soul in such a way that you will know without a doubt that there is a God in heaven Who loves you immeasurably.

"Allow Me to be the author of your life's story; I will not get it wrong—I know you better than you know yourself. Some things are not for you to know yet; that's where faith comes in—believe and receive. What I give you will never be less than what is needed to experience a life filled with wonder and awe, just as you were created to do for My glory."

Deut. 7:9 (NIV) ~ "Know therefore that the Lord your God is God; he is the faithful God, keeping his covenant of love to a thousand generations of those who love him and keep his commandments."

Me: "Lord, what do You want me to know today?"

God: "I have seen you falter in your walk with Me; that is why I always stay close beside you, so you will not fall. The enemy will attempt to trip you, time and again. Hold onto My hand, and you will have the strength to overcome adversity that might otherwise knock you down. Your story will be an inspiration to others when they see the positive results of a life lived in close relationship with Me."

John 16:33 (NIV) ~ "I have told you these things, so that in me you may have peace. In this world you will have trouble. But take heart! I have overcome the world."

Me: "Lord, what do You want me to know today?"

God: "What seems like an impossible situation to you is never impossible when I'm in control. I will work something good out of everything you go through. Your job is to be willing to be led by Me through the fire, with unwavering faith in My ability to ensure a good outcome for everyone involved.

"Rather than worrying about what you can't control, pray about everything and know that your prayers will make a difference; in fact, your prayers can move mountains. Never doubt what praying in Jesus' Name can and will accomplish."

Is. 43:2 (NIV) ~ "When you pass through the waters, I will be with you; and when you pass through the rivers, they will not sweep over you. When you walk through the fire, you will not be burned; the flames will not set you ablaze."

Me: "Lord, what do You want me to know today?"

God: "When you sense Me at work in your life, do not ignore it. Come to Me in humble submission and offer yourself to Me in every area of your life, that nothing else will take a position of more importance to you than your relationship with Me. Then you will know My good and perfect will, as I continue the good work I have begun in you. Let Me show you what true joy is when you walk closely with me."

Job 22:21-22 (NIV) ~ "Submit to God and be at peace with him; in this way prosperity will come to you. Accept instruction from his mouth and lay up his words in your heart."

Me: "Lord, what do You want me to know today?"

God: "The course I have laid out for your life will not always be easy to navigate, but there will be many rewarding moments and events along the way. I have given you the tenacity to survive and thrive in ways you never imagined possible. I have given you the strength to overcome adversity when you feel you are at your weakest.

"Keep leaning into Me, and talk to Me about everything as you move forward through each day. Keep reading My Word and get to know Me better; then you will find yourself trusting Me more and worrying less."

Is. 40:29 (NIV) ~ "He gives strength to the weary and increases the power of the weak."

Me: "Lord, what do You want me to know today?"

God: "I have heard your prayers on behalf of others and also yourself. I am working out My perfect will in each situation. Watch and see what I will do.

"Keep praying, and let Me control the outcomes. There is nothing too hard for Me to accomplish. Be certain that I have chosen to give you this responsibility because I know you are able to do it faithfully. Do not become lax in your prayer habits. Someone you know has a need I will answer as a result of your prayers said on their behalf."

Ps. 86:5 (NIV) ~ "You, Lord, are forgiving and good, abounding in love to all who call to you."

Me: "Lord, what do You want me to know today?"

God: "There is a reason for your time of waiting. I am preparing you for something you're not yet ready to do. You will find that your strength will come from Me, alone, when the time is right.

"As you wait on Me for guidance, let your heart not be troubled, but instead keep using your gifts and talents to minister to others. I will multiply your efforts even as I grow you in your faith and understanding of Who I am and what I am accomplishing in your life."

Ps. 27:14 (NIV) ~ "Wait for the Lord; be strong and take heart and wait for the Lord."

Me: "Lord, what do You want me to know today?"

God: "The more you read My Holy Word and come to understand My character and the immensity of My love for you, the more you will want to know Me. As you seek to know Me, the more of My glory I will show you.

"I have great plans for you. Let Me lead you in the way I know is best for you. When you can't understand where I'm taking you, simply trust Me and move forward in anticipation of what I am going to do; I will not disappoint you. Faith in My perfect timing will get you through any difficult situation you find yourself in. Remember where your strength comes from—I am here for you always."

Ps. 33:4-5 (NIV) ~ "For the word of the Lord is right and true; he is faithful in all he does. The Lord loves righteousness and justice; the earth is full of his unfailing love."

Me: "Lord, what do You want me to know today?"

God: "Meet with Me in prayer as you think about things that concern you. Offer up to Me your concerns and trust that I will handle them in such a way that you will no longer need to be burdened by them. You never need to feel powerless in any situation, because I've given you the power of prayer to use at any and all times to combat whatever assails you. Pray in Jesus' name and wait expectantly for Me to answer. Don't be surprised at what I will do in response.

"The better you know Me, the more you will take notice of all the ways I am at work in your life, and the more encouraged you will be. Be willing to share with others all that I've done, and am doing, in your life—thus boasting of Christ, and not of your own works, that I may be glorified by you all the days of your life."

Ps. 44:8 (NIV) ~ "In God we make our boast all day long, and we will praise your name forever."

Me: "Lord, what do You want me to know today?"

God: "Set your sights on what I've given you to accomplish, and I will help you complete the work. As you finish what I've given you to do, I will entrust you with other projects that I plan for you to complete for the furthering of My kingdom work on earth.

"You will know the joy of satisfaction as you work alongside Me, using the gifts and talents I gave you to carry out work that no one but you can do. My blessings for you cannot be compared to those I give anyone else, for only you are qualified to receive what I've set apart for you in accordance with your obedience to Me."

Col. 1:12 (NIV) ~ "and giving joyful thanks to the Father, who has qualified you to share in the inheritance of his holy people in the kingdom of light."

Me: "Lord, what do You want me to know today?"

God: "Look to the heavens when you need a reminder of My bountiful blessings to you. Try to count the stars, and try to count all your blessings—there are too many to count. I love you more than you can imagine. I am at work in your life right now, and My plan for you is very good. Walk closely with Me, and I will open your eyes to what I am doing.

"You have no need to fear your future, for I am already there ahead of you. I will light your way, that no darkness will befall you. Keep your eyes on Me and have the courage to enjoy the journey, no matter what I have planned for you. It will be amazing. Do you trust Me?"

Ps. 121:1-2 (NIV) ~ "I lift up my eyes to the mountains—where does my help come from? My help comes from the Lord, the Maker of heaven and earth."

Me: "Lord, what do You want me to know today?"

God: "Lessons come in all forms. When you don't understand why I am allowing you to go through certain circumstances, look for the lessons I want you to learn.

"Ask Me to show you what I am doing. Be ready to hear the hard things and be willing to be broken in the areas that need it in your life. Then I will heal your broken places in such a way that you will be made new, and I will be glorified in and through you as you willingly submit your whole heart into My hands on a daily basis."

Eph. 4:22-24 (NIV) ~ "You were taught, with regard to your former way of life, to put off your old self, which is being corrupted by its deceitful desires; to be made new in the attitude of your minds; and to put on the new self, created to be like God in true righteousness and holiness."

Me: "Lord, what do You want me to know today?"

God: "Open your heart daily to receive what I will reveal to you about yourself and My love for you. There will be times when you won't want to hear what I will tell you— listen to Me anyway, with all faith in My ability to ensure your continued growth in the areas of your life that you and I both know are in need of change.

"You will not look back with regret when you see what I have accomplished through your willingness to be compliant and submissive to My sovereign authority over your life. Don't miss out on all I intend for you to experience from the abundance of My love for you."

Dan. 2:22 (NIV) ~ "He reveals deep and hidden things; he knows what lies in darkness, and light dwells with him."

Me: "Lord, what do You want me to know today?"

God: "Do not settle for less than what I created you for. Do not sell yourself short. I have given you every ability you need to live a life of meaning and purpose that will change lives with a positive impact, which will astound and delight even yourself.

"Be willing to be stretched and shaped in ways that allow My light to shine out more brightly in your life, that others may see and believe that I am Who I say I am. As you follow My Divine plan for your life, you will experience joy, peace, and contentment like you've never known."

Ps. 51:12 (NIV) ~ "Restore to me the joy of your salvation and grant me a willing spirit, to sustain me."

September 15

Me: "Lord, what do You want me to know today?"

God: "Strive to be the kind of person you would trust with your heart and your life. Reach out to others with the same love I've shown to you. Make it your daily mission to encourage someone who crosses your mind or your path.

"You have the potential to make a difference of untold value in someone's life every day—step out of your comfort zone and be willing to be stretched when I present you with an opportunity to do so. There is nothing like the blessing of love being poured out from a sincere heart."

John 13:34-35 (NIV) ~ "A new command I give you: Love one another. As I have loved you, so you must love one another. By this everyone will know that you are my disciples, if you love one another."

Me: "Lord, what do You want me to know today?"

God: "Wherever you are right now is where I can carry out My perfect will in your life. What you need to do is trust Me with all your heart and believe that I do have a perfect plan for you. Don't try to figure out what needs to happen next. Move forward in completing what I've already given you to work on, and keep watching and listening for further instructions from Me. You will not miss My signals if you stay focused and alert at all times.

"Do not swerve to the right or the left when uncertainties cross your path—I will lead you right through them as you keep your eyes on Me. Read My Word diligently and talk to Me in prayer on a regular basis, and you will come to understand that you have no need to ever doubt My provision and care of you."

Ps. 91:2 (NIV) ~ "I will say of the Lord, 'He is my refuge and my fortress, my God, in whom I trust.'"

Me: "Lord, what do You want me to know today?"

God: "Those who choose to do life their own way will experience much unnecessary pain and suffering as a result of poor choices they will make along the way. On the other hand, all who heed My commands and seek My direction on a daily basis will know a peace unlike any other no matter what difficulties come their way, for I will uphold them and sustain them as I steady their feet and walk with them in the way they should go.

"When you put your trust fully in Me, you will see for yourself how trustworthy I am. Some things cannot be explained but must be experienced in order for you to understand."

Ps. 145:13 (NIV) ~ "Your kingdom is an everlasting kingdom, and your dominion endures through all generations. The Lord is trustworthy in all he promises and faithful in all he does."

Me: "Lord, what do You want me to know today?"

God: "Embrace those gifts and talents I've given you; do not set them aside to use at a later time—the time is now. Select something in your schedule to give up, so you can make more time to flourish in a God-centered way rather than a you-centered way, and focus on carrying out My kingdom purpose in your area of giftedness.

"What I ask you to do may be totally different than what you feel capable of doing—that's because I want you to learn to lean on Me for your strength and courage. Never doubt My ability and desire to accomplish great things of eternal significance through your sacrificial obedience to Me."

Ps. 115:14-15 (NIV) ~ "May the Lord cause you to flourish, both you and your children. May you be blessed by the Lord, the Maker of heaven and earth."

Me: "Lord, what do You want me to know today?"

God: "When I show you My will in different areas of your life, I expect you to follow through with what I indicate is necessary. Don't rely on your own reasoning—it cannot be trusted. Where there is doubt, there is a need for wisdom. Bring your doubts to Me, and let Me expose the truth to you in every situation.

"Don't move forward with any decision until I give you peace about the right thing to do. You are My beloved child; trust Me to lead you in the right direction."

Micah 6:8 (NIV) ~ "He has shown you, O mortal, what is good. And what does the Lord require of you? To act justly and to love mercy and to walk humbly with your God."

Me: "Lord, what do You want me to know today?"

God: "What seems like a hardship to you, waiting for My answer to your prayers, is something I want you to release into My hands. Don't hold onto it. Set your mind and your heart on doing what I've given you to do, as you leave the rest to Me.

"I am the One Who called you out of darkness into light, and I will prove My faithfulness to you over and over as you watch with wondering eyes. That's how much I love you."

2 Thess. 3:5 (NIV) ~ "May the Lord direct your hearts into God's love and Christ's perseverance."

Me: "Lord, what do You want me to know today?"

God: "There will be something each day that I have purposed for you to do. Be ready when I nudge you, for some things can't wait until you feel like doing them.

"I have given you an inheritance in My Kingdom through the blood of Christ poured out for your salvation. Be willing to share this wealth with anyone I send your way. Through your acts of selfless love, kindness, and generosity, others will witness My hand at work and will know they have not been forgotten or forsaken by Me. Hearts and lives continue to be touched and changed as a result of My children hearing and obeying what I ask them to do."

Col. 3:12 (NIV) ~ "Therefore, as God's chosen people, holy and dearly loved, clothe yourselves with compassion, kindness, humility, gentleness and patience."

Me: "Lord, what do You want me to know today?"

God: "My will for you is not always easy to discern on a day-to-day basis, but as you keep your eyes focused on what I am teaching you through My Holy Word and My answers to your prayers, you will see how I am involved in your life in a very personal way.

"I will remind you of those things I've already taught you, at the right times when you need to hear them again. Do not brush off these reminders as unimportant coincidences, but hold onto them and ponder them in your heart, even sharing them with others as I instruct you, for through your own experiences others may see and hear about My Divine interest in interacting closely with My beloved children. Never pass up an opportunity to share your Father's love with others."

Ps. 19:8 (NIV) ~ "The precepts of the Lord are right, giving joy to the heart. The commands of the Lord are radiant, giving light to the eyes."

Me: "Lord, what do You want me to know today?"

God: "Just as I have heard your heartfelt prayers, your cries of anguish, your shouts of joy, and your songs of praise, I have also heard your innermost thoughts, including your doubts and fears, your self-criticism, your angry feelings toward others, and everything else you keep locked away in your heart and mind.

"There is nothing that is hidden from Me and nothing that I can't help you overcome, or forgive you of. Lay all of it at My feet; surrender it all and let My peace wash over you and fill your empty places. Then you will know the fullness of My love for you and the capacity with which I created you to experience it. For no matter how deep your hurts may be, My love is deeper still."

Ps. 63:3 (NIV) ~ "Because your love is better than life, my lips will glorify you."

Me: "Lord, what do You want me to know today?"

God: "Submit to Me in every way I ask you to. Let My statutes be the foundation upon which you build your life. Don't listen when others mock you for being different. Instead, concentrate on those things I am teaching you that will become the signposts to lead you, and those impacted by your faith walk, in the way I want you to go.

"The steadfast heart will not be led astray by distractions of the world, but will hold fast to My life-giving, peace-infusing outpouring of love, grace, wisdom, and compassion offered freely to all who will receive it, and by doing so, will live 'in' the world, but not 'of' the world."

Deut. 10:20 (NIV) ~ "Fear the Lord your God and serve him. Hold fast to him and take your oaths in his name."

Me: "Lord, what do You want me to know today?"

God: "When waves of doubt and despair crash over you, I will help you stand firm. I am the One with the insight needed to help you move to higher ground when storms come your way. You don't have to flounder hopelessly; I will be your lifeline. Reach out to Me, and I will show you how strong My love for you is. I will never let you sink. Trusting Me in every situation takes courage—the more you practice, the stronger your faith will grow."

2 Cor. 4:8 (NIV) ~ "We are hard pressed on every side, but not crushed; perplexed, but not in despair;"

Me: "Lord, what do You want me to know today?"

God: "Seasons come and seasons go. Along with them come life, death, hope, and transformation. For believers, I have given My assurance that I will be with them always, in every situation they go through, and I will grow their faith in Me as they look beyond what they see and feel to focus on My sovereign hand at work in their lives through times of triumph and tribulation alike.

"I love My children with an everlasting love, and I want them to believe and understand this in such a way that it will change their lives, now and forever."

Ps. 73:25-26 (NIV) ~ "Whom have I in heaven but you? And earth has nothing I desire besides you. My flesh and my heart may fail, but God is the strength of my heart and my portion forever."

Me: "Lord, what do You want me to know today?"

God: "I have given you all the resources you need for the work I've called you to do at this time in your life. Let that be enough to keep you moving forward in obedience to Me.

"I will show you which direction to go—just keep moving, using all I've provided for you. Don't waste moments or days trying to figure out what will come next. Live in this moment, focusing your heart on walking closely with Me, so you will hear everything I am saying to you."

1 Cor. 4:2 (NIV) ~ "Now it is required that those who have been given a trust must prove faithful."

Me: "Lord, what do You want me to know today?"

God: "Your life is not defined by the rules you've been given to live by, or the rules you've created for yourself, but rather, by your response to the love I've given you, which comes from the depths of My heart. The way you respond to My love affects the way you respond to everything else in your life.

"When you freely received My love (through My Son, Jesus Christ, as your Savior and Lord) into your heart, I also gave you My Holy Spirit to live in you and guide you in the way you should go. Let Him do His work. Do not ignore Him when He nudges you to act or when He whispers a warning to keep you on the right track. I speak to you through My Holy Spirit, yet you still get to choose whether or not to listen and obey. Choose wisely, that others may see My hand at work in your life and respond to My love, themselves."

2 Cor. 3:17-18 (NIV) ~ "Now the Lord is the Spirit, and where the Spirit of the Lord is, there is freedom. And we all, who with unveiled faces contemplate the Lord's glory, are being transformed into his image with ever-increasing glory, which comes from the Lord, who is the Spirit."

Me: "Lord, what do You want me to know today?"

God: "Tend to the duties I've given you. Do this faithfully, and I will let you know when it's time for you to do something else. Let My provision for you be enough for the time being. Where I have you now is where I know you can be of the most benefit to the furthering of My kingdom work in your center of influence. I will continue to guide and strengthen you as you lean on Me and trust in My goodness for you."

Prov. 3:3 (NIV) ~ "Let love and faithfulness never leave you; bind them around your neck, write them on the tablet of your heart."

Me: "Lord, what do You want me to know today?"

God: "Being led by the Holy Spirit on a daily basis will cause your heart and mind to remain open to what I am doing in and through you to fulfill My purpose in your lifetime. Offer to Me your moments and your days, and ask Me to align them with My will for you. Then, move forward confidently, with the knowledge that your Creator will be personally involved in your day, directing your steps and rearranging your schedule when necessary, either for your own benefit or for the benefit of someone else whom I will use you to bless—sometimes without you even realizing it.

"Trust Me in all things without grumbling. I know what you need better than you do."

Rom. 8:14 (NIV) ~ "For those who are led by the Spirit of God are the children of God."

October 1

Me: "Lord, what do You want me to know today?"

God: "There is no one on earth who can love you like I do. My love for you is unsurpassable. Search your heart and mind daily to uncover and expose anything you harbor that has the potential of being detrimental to your relationship with Me. If it doesn't draw you toward Me, it will numb you toward Me.

"Each new day I wait for you with open arms, ready to sing My love song over you. When you spend time with Me in prayer, reading My Holy Word, and just sitting quietly in My presence, there is no end to what I will teach you about yourself, Myself, and the beauty of a lifetime spent walking closely with Me on a journey that will never cease to amaze you."

Ps. 89:1 (NIV) ~ "I will sing of the Lord's great love forever; with my mouth I will make your faithfulness known through all generations."

Me: "Lord, what do You want me to know today?"

God: "The remedy for your uncertainties in life is to spend more time with Me. You have questions, and I have answers. The more time you spend getting to know Me and learning to hear My voice, the easier it will be for you to discern when it is actually Me speaking to you, rather than your own thoughts you're hearing or lies of the enemy competing for your attention. When you truly want to know Me, I will make Myself known to you."

Deut. 4:29 (NIV) ~ "But if from there you seek the Lord your God, you will find him if you seek him with all your heart and with all your soul."

Me: "Lord, what do You want me to know today?"

God: "Whatever you choose to do at any given time will ultimately have some effect on your future choices, whether good or bad. When you ask Me for wisdom before you act on an inclination, don't move forward with a decision until I give you peace about it. Be willing to wait for My answer. I will let you know if there is a reason to rush into something; remember, I see the whole picture. Anything I want you to know will be made clear to you at the right time as you wait on Me to reveal it.

"Make time with Me a priority, and talk to Me often throughout your day. What is important to you is even more important to Me—that's how much I love you."

Ps. 38:15 (NIV) ~ "Lord, I wait for you; you will answer, Lord my God."

Me: "Lord, what do You want me to know today?"

God: "Close your eyes and think about a time when you had to depend on someone else to take care of you for whatever reason. Did you feel helpless, or did you feel comforted by knowing you were in the care of capable hands? Now, close your eyes and think back to a time when you knew without a doubt that My capable hands were holding you and caring for you during a time of fear, sorrow, or suffering. How did you know it was Me, and what was your response as a result of that knowledge?

"The more time you spend in close communion with Me, the more you will recognize My hand at work in your life, and the greater your faith in Me will become. When something amazes you, you want to share it with others. Let it be the same when you experience My goodness to you—do not keep it to yourself. Share it every chance you get, that others may know I'm here for them, also."

Ps. 23:6 (NIV) ~ "Surely your goodness and love will follow me all the days of my life, and I will dwell in the house of the Lord forever."

Me: "Lord, what do You want me to know today?"

God: "I have given you My Word as a promise of My love for you. When you read My Words of Life in the Holy Bible, your eyes will be opened to the immensity of My gift of grace poured out for you at Calvary through the blood of My Son, Jesus Christ.

"You will also come to know how deeply I value having a close, heart-to-heart relationship with you. I want to hear everything you will tell Me, good or bad. I want you to know that there is nothing beyond the reach of My forgiveness. Breathe deeply in My presence, and let My peace fill you as you relinquish all of your concerns into My hands. You are safe in My care."

Ps. 119:41 (NIV) ~ "May your unfailing love come to me, Lord, your salvation, according to your promise;"

Me: "Lord, what do You want me to know today?"

God: "Anyone can profess to believe in Me, but only those who have honestly repented of their sins and received My free gift of salvation will come to know Me as their Lord and Savior and be certain of eternal life with Me in heaven.

"Because you are My child, you are also My disciple. Let your life be a story that points others to My waiting arms, that none be lost for lack of obedience and fruitfulness on your part. You know that the things of the world will not satisfy a searching heart. Be the light in someone's darkness. Be brave and willing. I am always with you. When you hear My voice, go."

Ps. 63:3 (NIV) ~ "Because your love is better than life, my lips will glorify you."

Me: "Lord, what do You want me to know today?"

God: "When you take time to be still before Me, I know you are serious about honoring Me as your God and Savior. You acknowledge your need for Me through this act of humble submission.

"I will make Myself known to you without clanging cymbals, yet in a way that will speak loudly regarding your specific circumstances, so that you may know the extent of My love for you and be able to respond with thankfulness and praise. Whatever I ask of you will not be more than you are capable of doing as you lean on Me for strength. Spend time with Me, and trust Me to lead you in the way that is right for you."

Ps. 46:10 (NIV) ~ "He says, 'Be still, and know that I am God; I will be exalted among the nations, I will be exalted in the earth.'"

October 8

Me: "Lord, what do You want me to know today?"

God: "Serving Me is best done with a heart of gratitude. Look past those things that weigh you down, and choose joy as you consider that My ways are higher than your ways. You don't need to figure out why I ask you to serve others in certain ways; you just need to carry out the work and stay focused on My goodness to you.

"I see your heart, I see your abilities, and I know the plans I have for you. I also know who needs what you have to offer. Trust Me in every situation, and let Me decide what you can and cannot do."

Mark 10:45 (NIV) ~ "For even the Son of Man did not come to be served, but to serve, and to give his life as a ransom for many."

Me: "Lord, what do You want me to know today?"

God: "Sincerity of heart is an important factor in establishing the kinds of relationships that will make an eternal impact with those people I bring across your path during your lifetime. When you're willing to step outside of your comfort zone and into someone else's circle of brokenness, that is when you will discover the treasure of the Kingdom of God being revealed to you and through you. True treasure is not found in things of earthly value, but in loving relationships that nurture the strengths, abilities, and beauty I've planted in the hearts of men, women, and children, alike.

"Be willing to be a vessel poured out into the lives of others—a reflection of My love to those who are hurting. Some will come to realize their great value in My sight and will readily receive the gift of salvation I offer them through the death and resurrection of My Son, Jesus Christ."

Ps. 34:18 (NIV) ~ "The Lord is close to the brokenhearted and saves those who are crushed in spirit."

Me: "Lord, what do You want me to know today?"

God: "There will be opportunities to share My love with others every time you are in contact with people in any situation, personal or otherwise. Do not shrug off these opportunities, no matter how awkward they may seem at the time. A good word, spoken in a sincere and timely manner, can override a lifetime of destructive thought patterns and re-direct someone's wayward course.

"Let My truths roll off your tongue in love as a natural part of your conversations daily. The more you do this consciously, the more your words will build others up rather than tear them down."

Ps.145:21 (NIV) ~ "My mouth will speak in praise of the Lord. Let every creature praise his holy name for ever and ever."

Me: "Lord, what do You want me to know today?"

God: "Because you are My child, you are under My protection. The enemy may attack you from all sides, but I will uphold you with My mighty right hand. Your lips will praise My Name as you see what I am doing in your life for the purpose of restoring and transforming you into all I've called you to be.

"Do not be dismayed over things turning out differently than you planned. My ultimate good for you will be made evident as you witness My perfect plans coming to fruition for your pleasure and for My glory in your lifetime."

Ps. 63:8 (NIV) ~ "I cling to you; your right hand upholds me."

Me: "Lord, what do You want me to know today?"

God: "Timing, in any circumstance, will lead to likely success or failure, depending on whether the outcome is generated by foreknowledge or spontaneous emotion. When you come to Me with every concern you have, every decision you need to make, I will come alongside of you and help you discern the answers you need, while giving you the peace and confidence that will enable you to take the appropriate action necessary. When you can't discern My will for you, trust Me to guide your actions."

Ps. 31:3 (NIV) ~ "Since you are my rock and my fortress, for the sake of your name lead and guide me."

Me: "Lord, what do You want me to know today?"

God: "Come to Me in earnest surrender, laying down at My feet all those things that hinder you from being available to Me when I call you to work on what I've given you to complete for My kingdom purpose in your lifetime.

"Trust Me to help you handle those things that slow you down and trip you up. I have better plans for you than to leave you stuck in a rut of just surviving; let Me show you the greater things you can accomplish with the very resources I've already given you. What I'm looking for in you is a heart of humble submission, willing to be shaped and molded by My hand, so that you may become more usable to Me and more resilient for the journey I intend to take you on."

Ps. 84:12 (NIV) ~ "Lord Almighty, blessed is the one who trusts in you."

Me: "Lord, what do You want me to know today?"

God: "I know some things in your life are hard to under-stand—they seem beyond your comprehension. Those are the situations I want you to give over to Me, with all faith in My ability to produce the right outcome. You don't need to second-guess Me, wondering if I'll get it right; you just need to follow My leading and trust Me with your whole heart.

"Apply My Words of Truth to every circumstance that causes your faith to falter. Be bold in proclaiming victory in Christ Jesus over anything that threatens to defeat you. Know your place in My family—a child of the Most High God. I have called you out of darkness and into My glorious light. Keep your eyes on Me and move forward in confidence."

Ps. 18:28-29 (NIV) ~ "You, Lord, keep my lamp burning; my God turns my darkness into light. With your help I can advance against a troop; with my God I can scale a wall."

Me: "Lord, what do You want me to know today?"

God: "Set your heart and mind on the higher things I present to you through My Word, and through the preaching and teaching of those I've appointed to minister, in order that you may live an upright and obedient life of humble service and submission to Me. Let no one persuade you that there is a better way to achieve your goals and find true joy and peace than to do it hand-in-hand with Me, following My lead on the path I know is perfect for you.

"When you walk with Me in childlike faith, I will open your eyes to the wondrous things I am doing in your life. You will not miss out on sensational experiences—the things I have planned for you are greater than you can imagine. Trust Me. Let go. Surrender all and let Me show you what your greatest life looks like according to what I had in mind when I created you. Together you and I will soar."

Acts 2:25 (NIV) ~ "David said about him: 'I saw the Lord always before me. Because he is at my right hand, I will not be shaken.'"

Me: "Lord, what do You want me to know today?"

God: "Stand with those who are being persecuted for their faith in Me. Let your words become actions for the sake of My Gospel being preached to all nations. There are those who would hear and believe, but for the opposition standing in the way. Let nothing stop the efforts of My faithful servants in completing the tasks I've assigned to them.

"The greatest thing you can do until I direct you otherwise is to pray unrelentingly for every situation I place on your heart that needs heavenly intervention. Pray in the Name of My Son, Jesus Christ, with all faith that I will hear and answer. Heaven and earth will be moved through the prayers of My faithful children. Don't let any opportunity pass you by; I have equipped you for spiritual warfare—use the weapon."

Eph. 6:12-13 (NIV) ~ "For our struggle is not against flesh and blood, but against the rulers, against the authorities, against the powers of this dark world and against the spiritual forces of evil in the heavenly realms. Therefore put on the full armor of God, so that when the day of evil comes, you may be able to stand your ground, and after you have done everything, to stand."

Me: "Lord, what do You want me to know today?"

God: "Cover your family and friends in prayer every day. Be diligent in petitioning Me on their behalf, for you may be the only one praying for them. Pray also for the strangers you encounter each day, even though you know nothing of their circumstances. Your prayers may move mountains for someone who has lost all hope.

"Take your responsibility as My child seriously. My Son, Jesus Christ, was given and poured out for you, that you also may live given and poured out as a reflection of His love to those around you, even when they can't see it."

1 Tim. 2:1 (NIV) ~ "I urge, then, first of all, that petitions, prayers, intercession and thanksgiving be made for all people—"

Me: "Lord, what do You want me to know today?"

God: "Surely I will go ahead of you and make clear the path I intend for you to take. When you dust off your feet and get moving, you will see how I will help you gain momentum to not only endure the journey but to enjoy it to the fullest of your capacity as I created you to do.

"Trust Me with the gifts I've given you and offer them up to Me as a sacrifice; I will show you how to use them in ways that will draw others to respond to My love, even as you see more of My glory revealed to you while you flourish under My leadership and direction."

Prov. 4:18 (NIV) ~ "The path of the righteous is like the morning sun, shining ever brighter till the full light of day."

Me: "Lord, what do You want me to know today?"

God: "Renew your heart daily by coming to Me in humble submission. Confess your sins, and ask for My forgiveness. Look to Me for strength as you go about your day. Talk to Me every chance you get. Listen for My voice, and watch for My signs to you. Then you will come to know Me better and walk more sure-footedly on the path I'm taking you on.

"I have placed a heart of determination within you. Aim for a standard of excellence in those areas of your life that truly matter—your relationship with Me, your relationships with others, and your use of the gifts I've entrusted to you to be used faithfully for My glory."

Phil. 4:8 (NIV) ~ "Finally, brothers and sisters, whatever is true, whatever is noble, whatever is right, whatever is pure, whatever is lovely, whatever is admirable—if anything is excellent or praiseworthy—think about such things."

Me: "Lord, what do You want me to know today?"

God: "Whenever you sense Me at work in your life, do not resist Me. Instead, ask Me what I want you to know about the situation. I am restoring what the locusts have eaten, but I want your cooperation, for that is necessary in order that others may see and know that I am in the business of transforming hearts and lives.

"As you cooperate with Me, it will become evident to those who know you best that they are seeing the hand of God at work. Do not be afraid of being transparent before others as I complete My good work in you, for that is how they will see My glory exhibited through your humble submission to Me."

James 4:10 (NIV) ~ "Humble yourselves before the Lord, and he will lift you up."

Me: "Lord, what do You want me to know today?"

God: "Cleansing of the heart begins with repentance. When you come to Me in humble submission, I will receive your offering of self-sacrifice, and I will forgive your sins, and they will be no more. Because you have been washed and redeemed by the blood of the Lamb, you have all access to heaven through My Holy Spirit living and working in you, and through the power of Jesus' Name, by which you pray.

"Remember these things when you come under attack from the powers of darkness that seek to turn your face away from My light and My love. Call out to Me anytime, anywhere, and I will hear you, and I will be your strength."

Ps. 91:14 (NIV) ~ "'Because he loves me,' says the Lord, 'I will rescue him; I will protect him, for he acknowledges my name.'"

Me: "Lord, what do You want me to know today?"

God: "When I ask you to raise your standard of excellence in order to align with My perfect will for your life, will you be eager to comply, or will you grumble and complain about being stretched more than is comfortable for you? Where I have placed you at this time is exactly where I can use you for the furthering of My kingdom purpose on earth. Your cooperation with Me is vital to completing those tasks I've designed especially for you to carry out, and your willing heart is what I am waiting for."

Ps. 90:14 (NIV) ~ "Satisfy us in the morning with your unfailing love, that we may sing for joy and be glad all our days."

Me: "Lord, what do You want me to know today?"

God: "Sensitive hearts need sensitive understanding. When I connect you relationally with other people, there is a purpose for it. Always seek to learn My purpose before you simply discard a relationship with someone I've brought across your path. I've given you specific gifts that will enable you to minister to others in a way that only you can. I don't always give you a choice of whom you are to minister to, but I do give you the choice of responding to Me with a 'yes' or 'no'. When you trust My guidance in such matters, you will find the blessings to be immeasurable.

"Keep your eyes, ears, and heart wide open, so as to be alert to the ways I will call you to interact with others who are hurting and needy. Ask Me to supply you with the patience, compassion, and understanding necessary to reflect My love to those who often can't even see their own need for it."

1 Pet. 3:8 (NIV) ~ "Finally, all of you, be like-minded, be sympathetic, love one another, be compassionate and humble."

Me: "Lord, what do You want me to know today?"

God: "Whatever must be done in your lifetime to fulfill the greatest purpose I created you for will be what I will call you to, again and again, until it is completed. Even when you can't envision all I have planned for you, stay the course, and I will reveal to you what is most necessary for you to know along the way. Trust My Divine wisdom and finish well, all while keeping your eyes and heart focused on Me as you follow My leading."

2 Pet. 1:10-11 (NIV) ~ "Therefore, my brothers and sisters, make every effort to confirm your calling and election. For if you do these things, you will never stumble, and you will receive a rich welcome into the eternal kingdom of our Lord and Savior Jesus Christ."

Me: "Lord, what do You want me to know today?"

God: "Satisfy yourself in My presence. What you most thirst for cannot be found in people or things of the world. Your deepest desire can only be satisfied in close communion with Me on a regular basis. I created you. I am the Lover of Your Soul. Come to Me with arms wide open; I will comfort you and be your strength. There is no situation that My steadfast love can't overcome in your life."

Ps. 91:15-16 (NIV) ~ "He will call on me, and I will answer him; I will be with him in trouble, I will deliver him and honor him. With long life I will satisfy him and show him my salvation."

Me: "Lord, what do You want me to know today?"

God: "When you abstain from participating in activities that do not honor Me, you show Me that your love for Me is greater than your love for the world. I created you with certain gifts and talents in order that you could glorify Me in your own unique way while also deriving great joy, peace, and satisfaction from your accomplishments.

"If you allow the constant lures of the world to distract you from the path I am leading you on, you will become hardened and empty, and no longer able to discern that which is displeasing in My sight. Therefore, guard your heart and mind through the choices you make and by coming to Me daily in repentance and humble submission. I will show you how to live your best life and how to live it abundantly, according to My perfect will for you."

Prov. 4:23 (NIV) ~ "Above all else, guard your heart, for everything you do flows from it."

Me: "Lord, what do You want me to know today?"

God: "I am pruning you so that you may produce more fruit for My kingdom purpose on earth. The more you cooperate with Me, the more you will see and understand what I am accomplishing in your life, and the beauty of it will be a testament to you of how much I love you and why I created you the way I did."

John 15:4 (NIV) ~ "Remain in me, as I also remain in you. No branch can bear fruit by itself; it must remain in the vine. Neither can you bear fruit unless you remain in me."

Me: "Lord, what do You want me to know today?"

God: "Most of your aspirations come from the wellspring of intellect and creativity I gave you when I formed you. You have natural tendencies that cause you to gravitate toward this inclination or that avenue of pursuit. The difference in where you'll end up, and the amount of joy and satisfaction you will experience, will depend on whether you are seeking to glorify yourself or to glorify Me by using what I've given you to enjoy and express yourself with."

Ps. 43:4 (NIV) ~ "Then I will go to the altar of God, to God, my joy and my delight. I will praise you with the lyre, O God, my God."

Me: "Lord, what do You want me to know today?"

God: "Gather your most treasured memories from the years of life I've given you, and consider what makes those memories so special to you. Can you see My fingerprints all over those situations? I was there with you, loving you, caring for you.

"I am always with you, and I still love you and care for you in ways you can't even imagine. Remember to look for Me in your moments and your days—look for what I am doing in your life; don't miss the signs and the blessings, even in times of hardship. Commit your days into My safekeeping, and ask Me to show you more of My glory; I will answer."

Ps. 139:17-18 (NIV) ~ "How precious to me are your thoughts, God! How vast is the sum of them! Were I to count them, they would outnumber the grains of sand—when I awake, I am still with you."

Me: "Lord, what do You want me to know today?"

God: "Consider what I've taught you about distractions and temptations of the world that draw your focus away from Me and the work I've called you to complete for the furthering of My Kingdom on earth. Which things in your life are darkening your heart and cluttering your mind, making you less useful for what I created you to accomplish in your lifetime? What will you do to change your situation?

"Ask Me for help and respond to My nudges when I point you in the way you should go. I will help you live your best life, but I want your cooperation and your full trust in My Divine wisdom and love."

1 John 2:15-16 (NIV) ~ "Do not love the world or anything in the world. If anyone loves the world, love for the Father is not in them. For everything in the world—the lust of the flesh, the lust of the eyes, and the pride of life—comes not from the Father but from the world."

Me: "Lord, what do You want me to know today?"

God: "When I call you to obey Me in any specific situation in your life, there is no 'maybe' about it. I want your full cooperation. I want your complete trust in My ability to work out the details as I know will be best for you and any others involved.

"Just do your part, and obey what I instruct you to do. Don't question My plan or suggest to others what they should do. Your obedience is a key piece of the whole picture."

Jer. 7:23 (NIV) ~ "but I gave them this command: Obey me, and I will be your God and you will be my people. Walk in obedience to all I command you, that it may go well with you."

Me: "Lord, what do You want me to know today?"

God: "Refuse to worry about the things you can't control. Let Me work out the details. I don't need your advice—I just want your obedience. Pray for My will to be done, and then let Me do it. Ask Me to teach you what I want you to know and be willing to adapt to change if I call you to do so.

"I created you specifically for a journey that only you can take in your days of life on this earth. I will be with you every step of the way. Be watchful, but not worried. Look for the blessings along the way, and consider whom you might share them with so as to brighten someone's day. I have called you to share My light and love with the people I've placed in your life. Don't let anything get in the way of doing that. Obey. Simply obey."

Matt. 6:34 (NIV) ~ "Therefore do not worry about tomorrow, for tomorrow will worry about itself. Each day has enough trouble of its own."

Me: "Lord, what do You want me to know today?"

God: "Hearing My voice and obeying what I ask of you will bring you into a closer relationship with Me and a greater understanding of My love for you.

"When you truly desire to know Me, I will make Myself known to you. Practice being still before Me and ask Me to reveal to you the things I want you to know. I take pleasure in conversing with you, and I want you to talk with Me throughout your day—even if it's a quiet prayer. The more you listen for My voice, the more you will learn to recognize Me when I speak to you, and the more joy you will discover, which I've been waiting to share with you."

Is. 6:8 (NIV) ~ "Then I heard the voice of the Lord saying, 'Whom shall I send? And who will go for us?' And I said, 'Here am I. Send me!'"

Me: "Lord, what do You want me to know today?"

God: "Carry My Word in your heart. Memorize My promises and meditate on them often, reciting them out loud to remind yourself and others of My faithfulness at all times and in all situations.

"When you have doubts or fears, My Words of Truth will bolster your confidence in My ability to lovingly care for you and handle whatever you're going through as you submit everything into My hands."

Ps. 119:11 (NIV) ~ "I have hidden your word in my heart that I might not sin against you."

Me: "Lord, what do You want me to know today?"

God: "When you acknowledge Me as the One Who provides all you need and much more, you will experience true contentment, no matter what your current situation is. There is nothing good that I will withhold from you when I know it will benefit your ability to complete all I've created you to do for My glory in your lifetime.

"I intend for you to experience the fullness of My love for you in the ways I will bless the works of your hands and the desires of your heart as you commit everything into My safekeeping and trust Me to guide your way."

Eph. 3:19 (NIV) ~ "and to know this love that surpasses knowledge—that you may be filled to the measure of all the fullness of God."

Me: "Lord, what do You want me to know today?"

God: "Look for signs of what I am doing in your life each day. Some days may feel just like the day before, but they are not. My mercies are new every morning. What I am accomplishing in your life will be a continually progressive shaping of your heart to conform with My perfect will for you, in accordance with how I created you in My own image.

"The more you become aware of My Presence with you at all times, the more you will see My hand at work in your every situation. Keep your eyes and your heart open. My glory will be revealed to you that you may rejoice in My sovereign love for you."

Lam. 3:22-23 (NIV) ~ "Because of the Lord's great love we are not consumed, for his compassions never fail. They are new every morning; great is your faithfulness."

Me: "Lord, what do You want me to know today?"

God: "Aim for righteousness in everything you do—even in your daily tasks, that your work would always point to the One Who gave you the ability to do the work, and not to yourself. You are to be a reflection of My love to the world.

"Don't let your attitudes or insecurities tarnish the reflection others will see when they observe you in action. When you lean on Me for strength at all times, I will help you be the best version of you, that you may shine for My glory."

Prov. 21:21 (NIV) ~ "Whoever pursues righteousness and love finds life, prosperity and honor."

Me: "Lord, what do You want me to know today?"

God: "Beneath the wound of heartache is new hope waiting to break through and flourish. As you walk with Me daily, I will reveal to you the areas of your heart that still need to be surrendered to Me so that you may experience My beautiful transformation work being made complete in your life. The more transparent you become with Me, the more peace, joy, and freedom you will feel as you let Me carry your burdens."

Rom. 6:13 (NIV) ~ "Do not offer any part of yourself to sin as an instrument of wickedness, but rather offer yourselves to God as those who have been brought from death to life; and offer every part of yourself to him as an instrument of righteousness."

Me: "Lord, what do You want me to know today?"

God: "Settle your anxious thoughts by giving them to Me every time you find yourself dwelling on them. I have better things for you to do with your time that will produce good fruits in your life and the lives of others.

"Concentrate on using your energy to complete the tasks I've given you to do. If you don't know what those are, ask Me for clarification and watch for My signs to you. When you truly seek to know My will, through reading My Word and through personal interaction with Me in prayer, I will not withhold from you anything necessary for the continued growth of your faith in My ability to guide you and shape you in the way you should go."

Job 42:2 (NIV) ~ "I know that you can do all things; no purpose of yours can be thwarted."

Me: "Lord, what do You want me to know today?"

God: "Simply let go of trying to be in control. Let Me show you how freeing it is when you no longer bear the weight of things you weren't meant to carry. Then you will know that My grace is sufficient for your needs, whatever they may be because I will show Myself faithful in ways you couldn't see before, while your eyes were on yourself."

Ps. 115:1 (NIV) ~ "Not to us, Lord, not to us but to your name be the glory, because of your love and faithfulness."

Me: "Lord, what do You want me to know today?"

God: "Know with certainty that I love you and am for you. I have given you many promises to this effect in My Holy Word.

"There is nothing I won't help you accomplish when I am invited into the midst of all you're attempting to do for My glory with the gifts and talents I've given you. Pray about everything, and keep moving forward. I will walk with you and direct your steps."

Jer. 29:12 (NIV) ~ "Then you will call on me and come and pray to me, and I will listen to you."

Me: "Lord, what do You want me to know today?"

God: "Resist taking matters with questionable outcomes into your own hands before bringing them to Me in prayer. How often My children rush headlong into something without thoroughly covering it in prayer first.

"Be willing to wait for My goodness to be shown to you and poured out upon you. I know what you need and when you need it. Your time of waiting will not be without good purpose. Keep your eyes focused on Me, and I will show you things about yourself that will reveal your need for My transforming power to cleanse and restore you. Be willing to be transparent, and let My glory be revealed in you and through you for the sake of My kingdom purpose for your life."

Ps. 37:4-6 (NIV) ~ "Take delight in the Lord, and he will give you the desires of your heart. Commit your way to the Lord; trust in him and he will do this: He will make your righteous reward shine like the dawn, your vindication like the noonday sun."

Me: "Lord, what do You want me to know today?"

God: "Turn your eyes on Me when doubts, fears, or temptations come your way. Ask Me for help right away —don't try to handle it in your own strength, or reason away the need to involve Me in the situation. I care about everything you face moment-by-moment. I will help you handle anything you encounter. Will you trust Me?

"Let Me give you My peace as you walk closely with Me each day. There will be no mountain in your way that can't be conquered when you team up with Me to face it head-on."

1 Chron. 16:11 (NIV) ~ "Look to the Lord and his strength; seek his face always."

Me: "Lord, what do You want me to know today?"

God: "Certainly, there will be times when you will feel far away from Me, but I will still be right here with you. That is where faith comes in; remember how I've walked with you this far. I will never leave you or forsake you. I am still finishing the good work I started in you.

"Pain is inevitable in a sinful world. How you react to it will either speed or slow your healing. Bring everything to Me in prayer. I will hear you, and I will sustain you as you wait on Me to answer."

Ps. 55:22 (NIV) ~ "Cast your cares on the Lord and he will sustain you; he will never let the righteous be shaken."

Me: "Lord, what do You want me to know today?"

God: "Trusting Me will sometimes be very difficult for you. When it's hardest for you to trust what I am doing in your particular situation, that is when your faith must be strongest for the sake of My glory being revealed in you and through you as you wait on Me to make known My will for you.

"Never underestimate the magnitude of all that I am accomplishing in your life and the lives of others as you wait on Me to reveal My purpose and affirm your faith in My timing."

Ps. 62:1-2 (NIV) ~ "Truly my soul finds rest in God; my salvation comes from him. Truly he is my rock and my salvation; he is my fortress, I will never be shaken."

Me: "Lord, what do You want me to know today?"

God: "Whenever you ask Me to show you My will for you, make sure you are open to whatever response I give you. The 'how' and 'when' of all I plan for you are not as important as the 'what'. Will you trust Me when My plans don't match up with yours? I know the desires of your heart and how I will blend them with My plans for you.

"When you surrender your dreams into My care, there will be no need to wonder at the outcome. Keep moving forward, doing what you know you are able to do right now. I will let you know when you need to shift directions. Let Me determine the timeline you will follow, in order that you may experience My greatest blessings that are still ahead for you."

Ps. 20:7 (NIV) ~ "Some trust in chariots and some in horses, but we trust in the name of the Lord our God."

Me: "Lord, what do You want me to know today?"

God: "Loosen your hold on whatever it is you're gripping more tightly than My truths that you hold in your heart. Surrender your biggest doubts and fears to Me daily. I will receive your offering of surrender, and will, in turn, give you My peace.

"There is nothing that can stand in the way of all the good I have in store for you as you cooperate with Me in every area of your life. Bit by bit, as you keep moving forward with Me in faith, you will see My transforming power making something beautiful out of all you've entrusted into My hands. I will be glorified through your humble submission to Me."

Ps. 31:19 (NIV) ~ "How abundant are the good things that you have stored up for those who fear you, that you bestow in the sight of all, on those who take refuge in you."

Me: "Lord, what do You want me to know today?"

God: "Stand on the promises of My Holy Word—read them, memorize them, speak them often, believe them, share them with others, pray them out loud for yourself and for others. Be ever watchful to see how these promises are being fulfilled in your life.

"My glory is all around you. You are always in My presence. The more you know Me, the more you will feel Me at work in your life, which will enable you to better reflect My glory to those around you."

Ps. 119:140 (NIV) ~ "Your promises have been thoroughly tested, and your servant loves them."

Me: "Lord, what do You want me to know today?"

God: "Beginning with those closest to you, leave no stone unturned in sharing My Gospel message. Ask the tough questions and be generous in your outpouring of love and grace, that others may see My transforming power at work in your life. Yes, this may be uncomfortable for you, but I won't ask you to do anything that I don't plan to help you accomplish. Submit everything to Me in prayer and let Me lead you in the way you should go."

1 Thess. 2:8 (NIV) ~ "so we cared for you. Because we loved you so much, we were delighted to share with you not only the gospel of God but our lives as well."

Me: "Lord, what do You want me to know today?"

God: "Seek Me with all sincerity, and you will know Me. Reorder your priorities so that I will be at the top of your list. Then you will see how everything else will fall into proper perspective as you acknowledge My rightful place in your heart and your life.

"Give Me the chance to show you how well My plans for you will mesh with your own dreams when you offer them up to Me in childlike faith. My love for you will always remain steadfast. Will you offer Me the same?"

Ps. 89:2 (NIV) ~ "I will declare that your love stands firm forever, that you have established your faithfulness in heaven itself."

Me: "Lord, what do You want me to know today?"

God: "Security is something you desire. I sent My Son into the world to die for your sins so that you could be secure in My love for you. This eternal love, this salvation bought with the blood of Christ, gives you more security than anything the world can offer.

"I will supply all your needs according to My perfect will for you. Trust Me in all things and go about the work I gave you to do. Commit each day into My safekeeping, and refuse to worry about anything. I will uphold you with My right hand, and you will be in My continuous care."

Ps. 16:5 (NIV) ~ "Lord, you alone are my portion and my cup; you make my lot secure."

Me: "Lord, what do You want me to know today?"

God: "Persevere when trials come, by looking to Me as the source of your strength. I knew you before I formed you in the womb, and I love you with an everlasting love.

"Nothing you go through is unnoticed by Me. Search your heart daily and expose to Me those areas that hinder you from walking in complete obedience to Me. Surrender those things to Me and receive My peace in exchange. Your heart is safe in My hands."

Rom. 5:3-4 (NIV) ~ "Not only so, but we also glory in our sufferings, because we know that suffering produces perseverance; perseverance, character; and character, hope."

Me: "Lord, what do You want me to know today?"

God: "Center your thoughts on My steadfast love for you. Memorize My promises to you and carry them in your heart. Speak them out loud with good purpose, on your own behalf, and the behalf of others, that the power of My Spirit in you may be made evident for the glory of My Holy Name."

Ps. 145:4-6 (NIV) ~ "One generation commends your works to another; they tell of your mighty acts. They speak of the glorious splendor of your majesty—and I will meditate on your wonderful works. They tell of the power of your awesome works—and I will proclaim your great deeds."

Me: "Lord, what do You want me to know today?"

God: "Just as there is a need for salvation for every sinner, there is also a need for understanding in the hearts of all who do not know Me. My children are called to be vessels of love and light to those lost in darkness.

"Do not sidestep those unsaved souls in your life. Instead, draw from the wellspring of My love for you, and likewise, extend this love to others, no matter how undeserving or unthankful they may seem. Let Me be in charge of the outcome—your job is to love faithfully and sincerely."

Rom. 12:9 (NIV) ~ "Love must be sincere. Hate what is evil; cling to what is good."

Me: "Lord, what do You want me to know today?"

God: "Furiously, the battle rages on while you are unaware—the battle between light and darkness. Your prayers make a powerful difference in the lives of many people who need them said on their behalf. I hear the prayers of My children, and I do answer them.

"When you take time to pray, you not only honor Me as the One Who is in control of all things but also you practice selfless love for others, as Christ modeled for you. The more you do this, the more natural it will become for you, and the more you will see My glory as you watch and wait for My answers to your prayers."

2 Cor. 1:10-11 (NIV) ~ "He has delivered us from such a deadly peril, and he will deliver us again. On him we have set our hope that he will continue to deliver us, as you help us by your prayers. Then many will give thanks on our behalf for the gracious favor granted us in answer to the prayers of many."

Me: "Lord, what do You want me to know today?"

God: "Abide in My love, for it is enough to sustain you through any trials that come your way. Hand your troubles over to Me and receive My Divine peace in return. Resist the temptation to dwell on matters you've already entrusted to Me—don't go there again.

"Begin each day with a fresh outlook and ask Me to direct your path. Then, move ahead in confidence, with eyes and ears alert to what I am doing in and through your life. You won't want to miss even the smallest encouragement I send your way."

2 Cor. 12:9 (NIV) ~ "But he said to me, 'My grace is sufficient for you, for my power is made perfect in weakness.' Therefore I will boast all the more gladly about my weaknesses, so that Christ's power may rest on me."

Me: "Lord, what do You want me to know today?"

God: "Common sense has a good purpose in your life, but it won't save your soul. There is nothing common about My Son, Jesus Christ, dying on the cross to save you from your sins. The more you read My Word and converse with Me through prayer, the more you will come to know and understand Me and the miracle of My greatest gift to you.

"I am doing miracles in your life every day. The more you watch for them, the more you will notice them. Some would brush off My miracles as mere coincidences, but you know better. You have seen My hand at work in your life many times, and your faith in Me has grown because of it. Keep your eyes open, that you may see more of My glory on a daily basis and realize how limitless My love for you truly is."

Job 9:10 (NIV) ~ "He performs wonders that cannot be fathomed, miracles that cannot be counted."

Me: "Lord, what do You want me to know today?"

God: "Success is highly valued in this world, but the way people view it varies greatly. When I gave you certain gifts and talents, I intended for you to use them for your enjoyment and fulfillment, and also for My glory.

"When you seek success with selfish motives, unhealthy pride tends to grow and flourish. On the other hand, where there is a humble heart toward God and man, the joy of serving will overshadow the need for recognition. Do not hesitate to use your gifts in any way I ask of you. Trust Me to help you achieve what you're meant to on earth, while you store up treasure in heaven through your faithful obedience to My calling."

Prov. 2:7 (NIV) ~ "He holds success in store for the upright, he is a shield to those whose walk is blameless,"

Me: "Lord, what do You want me to know today?"

God: "Stand your ground when the enemy attacks. Pray in the Name of Jesus, and your foe will have to leave.

"Be the prayer warrior in your family—don't wait for someone else to take responsibility for upholding those you love in prayer on a continual basis. The more you pray, the more you will understand the necessity of it, and the power of My Holy Name will become more evident to you through the ways I answer your prayers."

Eph. 6:10-11 (NIV) ~ "Finally, be strong in the Lord and in his mighty power. Put on the full armor of God, so that you can take your stand against the devil's schemes."

Me: "Lord, what do You want me to know today?"

God: "Release into My care every burden you struggle with. There is no reason to hold onto things you can't control. I placed the stars in the heavens and named every one of them. I set the earth into motion, and it continues thus today.

"I want you to trust Me completely in every situation. I can see things you cannot. I have knowledge that you will never have. My love for you stretches throughout eternity. I hold your future in My hands and have given you life with the intent that you enjoy it. When you walk closely with Me, you have no reason to be afraid. I am the Giver and Sustainer of Life."

Ps. 147:4-5 (NIV) ~ "He determines the number of the stars and calls them each by name. Great is our Lord and mighty in power; his understanding has no limit."

Me: "Lord, what do You want me to know today?"

God: "There is never a wrong time to call out to Me in prayer. It can be as simple as, 'Help, Lord!'. When your heart is sincere, I will hear you, and I will help you. Even if you have just a few seconds to acknowledge Me and call out to Me, do it. Get in the habit of talking to Me, first, in every situation you face, good or bad; this will remind you that I am with you always.

"The more you rely on My strength, the easier your day will go, and the more you will be able to pour out My love into the lives of others. I will enable you to live 'given and poured out' in such a way that your cup will never run dry."

Ps. 18:6 (NIV) ~ "In my distress I called to the Lord; I cried to my God for help. From his temple he heard my voice; my cry came before him, into his ears."

Me: "Lord, what do You want me to know today?"

God: "Stand up for all that you know is right and just, according to what is written in My Holy Word. I have called you to be My ambassador; do not take this calling lightly. Do everything in love, seasoned with confidence in My ability to help you as you share the reasons for your faith with others.

"When someone is hurting, give them more than a pat on the back—be the hands and feet of Christ. Ask Me to help you and follow My nudging. Then, even if you fail to comfort them, you will not have failed Me, and I will multiply your efforts to produce fruit for My Kingdom, in My perfect timing."

Luke 8:15 (NIV) ~ "But the seed on good soil stands for those with a noble and good heart, who hear the word, retain it, and by persevering produce a crop."

Me: "Lord, what do You want me to know today?"

God: "Waste no time on trivial things that have no purpose toward helping you grow spiritually. Your time on earth is limited—spend it with the intent of investing in kingdom treasure, not worldly fancies. Yes, I created the world for you to enjoy, and I placed people in your life so you could learn to love and be loved. All this I did with the love of a Father toward His children, that you may reflect My glory to those who do not yet know Me.

"Don't follow the patterns of the world. Do not be content to settle for less when I have so much more for you. There is no joy possible that can compare to the joy I give My children when they come to know Me, personally, as their God and Savior. Allow that joy to overflow in your life, through love and kindness toward others, and you will reap more blessings than you give in your remaining days on this earth."

Ps. 119:111-112 (NIV) ~ "Your statutes are my heritage forever; they are the joy of my heart. My heart is set on keeping your decrees to the very end."

Me: "Lord, what do You want me to know today?"

God: "Shoulder the burdens of others with grace when I ask you to. If they seem unthankful, remember that I see everything and will reward you accordingly. When your heart is set on serving Me through serving others, the tasks become more joy-filled, and you will better recognize My hand at work, supplying all you need for completing whatever I call you to do."

1 Thess. 5:11 (NIV) ~ "Therefore encourage one another and build each other up, just as in fact you are doing."

Me: "Lord, what do You want me to know today?"

God: "Dearly beloved child of Mine, it is not for you to know yet all that I have planned for your lifetime on earth. Just know that whatever I ask you to do on any given day is part of the whole beautiful picture of your life's puzzle that is coming together in My perfect timing.

"I will not let your story end before it is finished. All the pieces of your life's picture will be in place before I call you home. Trust Me to help you finish well. There is no need to second-guess the path when you let Me be your guide. I am here, I am for you, and I love you more than you can imagine."

Ps. 100:3 (NIV) ~ "Know that the Lord is God. It is he who made us, and we are his; we are his people, the sheep of his pasture."

Me: "Lord, what do You want me to know today?"

God: "Let Me guide not only your path but also your conversations with others along the way. Choose your words carefully, speak My truth in love whenever I give you an opportunity, and talk about your blessings more than your disappointments. In this way, you will point others to the true source of joy, peace, love, and grace, given and poured out for you at Calvary—Jesus Christ, The Way, The Truth, and The Life."

Ps. 19:14 (NIV) ~ "May these words of my mouth and this meditation of my heart be pleasing in your sight, Lord, my Rock and my Redeemer."

Me: "Lord, what do You want me to know today?"

God: "Hold on to the things I teach you, and treasure them in your heart. Apply them to your life circumstances every chance you get. You are My ambassador and a role model for all who are watching you. Let it not be said of you that you rebelled against the God you serve. Live your life as a testimony of My great love for you, and trust Me in everything. I am with you always."

Titus 2:11-12 (NIV) ~ "For the grace of God has appeared that offers salvation to all people. It teaches us to say 'No' to ungodliness and worldly passions, and to live self-controlled, upright and godly lives in this present age,"

Me: "Lord, what do You want me to know today?"

God: "Share with Me everything in your heart on a daily basis. Be willing to be transparent. Offer your gifts and talents to Me every day, and ask Me to show you how to use them for My glory. Be willing to rearrange your plans if I require it of you. I see things you can't even imagine, and I will put you in the right place at the right time as you humbly and patiently submit to My leading."

Luke 9:23 (NIV) ~ "Then he said to them all: 'Whoever wants to be my disciple must deny themselves and take up their cross daily and follow me."

Me: "Lord, what do You want me to know today?"

God: "I have given you the resources and abilities you need to continue moving forward with the work I've called you to do. Keep at it, and don't worry about tomorrow, the next day, or the next. I will provide all you need in ways you can't yet see, as you keep leaning on Me for strength and trusting My perfect timing.

"There is no better time than now to embrace the adventure I have planned for you and to discover the greater purposes I've placed in your heart that will draw you closer to My own heart in so many beautiful ways. Will you take that next step of faith?"

Prov. 4:11-12 (NIV) ~ "I instruct you in the way of wisdom and lead you along straight paths. When you walk, your steps will not be hampered; when you run, you will not stumble."

Me: "Lord, what do You want me to know today?"

God: "Walk in the way of righteousness in all you do. I will help you overcome whatever stands in your way so that you may keep moving forward with Me along the path I have designed just for you.

"Seek to know My will daily, and I will open your eyes to see the things that matter most in your life. There will be nothing that can stop My hand from leading you in the way you should go when you keep your eyes and your heart fixed on Me."

Ps. 1:1 (NIV) ~ "Blessed is the one who does not walk in step with the wicked or stand in the way that sinners take or sit in the company of mockers,"

Me: "Lord, what do You want me to know today?"

God: "Look to My Word when you have questions about what is happening in your life and what you can expect Me to do about it. Ask Me to teach you what I want you to know, and submit yourself humbly and willingly to My leadership. Ask yourself what is getting in the way between you and Me when you have difficulty surrendering to My will for your life. Then, allow Me to lead you in the way of wisdom so that you may experience freedom from the strongholds, idols, and addictions the enemy wants to snare you with.

"You are My child, called to live in victory. Don't settle for anything less than My best plans for you."

Gal. 5:1 (NIV) ~ "It is for freedom that Christ has set us free. Stand firm, then, and do not let yourselves be burdened again by a yoke of slavery."

Me: "Lord, what do You want me to know today?"

God: "Confidence in My love for you and My ability to lead you through any situation at any time is what will keep you moving forward when you might otherwise give up. Remember all I've brought you through so far, and keep standing on the promises I've given you in My Holy Word.

"Speak of My glory every chance you get, and be willing to come alongside others who are suffering, for in doing so you may bless them in such a way that they will see My hand at work in their lives, also. Your willingness to serve Me, even in difficult situations, is evidence of your love for Me. As you love the people I've placed in your life, you are also loving Me."

Ps. 71:5 (NIV) ~ "For you have been my hope, Sovereign Lord, my confidence since my youth."

Me: "Lord, what do You want me to know today?"

God: "Run to Me when you feel the lure of sin and darkness threatening to pull you away from the light of My love. My Holy Spirit living in you will warn you when you're entering dangerous territory. Listen to the Voice of Truth, and obey My warnings. In this way, you will avoid much unnecessary heartache and sorrow."

1 John 1:6 (NIV) ~ "If we claim to have fellowship with him and yet walk in the darkness, we lie and do not live out the truth."

Me: "Lord, what do You want me to know today?"

God: "Those who look to Me for understanding and call upon Me for wisdom will receive instruction and discernment as needed while I lead them in the way they should go. I will never forget your cries for help and will continue to be with you all along the journey of your lifetime.

"You cannot see what lies ahead, so trust the One Who can. Walk closely with Me, and I will teach you amazing things you would never see or comprehend on your own. I delight in sharing My heart with you."

Ps. 16:7 (NIV) ~ "I will praise the Lord, who counsels me; even at night my heart instructs me."

Me: "Lord, what do You want me to know today?"

God: "There is none who can finish the work I've given you to do—none but yourself. Therefore, you needn't compare yourself to anyone, because what I've given you is yours alone to complete for My glory in your lifetime.

"You never need to bear the weight of comparison, for it has no jurisdiction over you unless you allow it to. You are free to be all I've created you to be within the boundaries I've set for you for your own good. As you honor Me with your time and your talents, I will sustain you and refresh you one day at a time."

Heb. 10:36 (NIV) ~ "You need to persevere so that when you have done the will of God, you will receive what he has promised."

Me: "Lord, what do You want me to know today?"

God: "Commit your moments and your days into My safekeeping. Then, live your life in full confidence in My ability to orchestrate your activities and associations in such a way that what's important will always get done, according to My perfect will for you.

"In other words, I will order your days accordingly, for the glory of My Holy Name, when you surrender your willfulness into My hands and submit to following My leading with a willing heart, day after day."

Jer. 17:7-8 (NIV) ~ "'But blessed is the one who trusts in the Lord, whose confidence is in him. They will be like a tree planted by the water that sends out its roots by the stream. It does not fear when heat comes; its leaves are always green. It has no worries in a year of drought and never fails to bear fruit.'"

Me: "Lord, what do You want me to know today?"

God: "Spend your time wisely, and waste no time fretting over what you can't control. Focus on doing what I've placed on your heart, even when it doesn't make sense from your human perspective.

"I am laying out the pieces of your life in the order they should go, according to My perfect plan for you. When you let go of that which you want to see happen next in your life, I will show you where it fits into My plan for you in a way that will delight you and glorify My Name at the same time."

Ps. 39:4 (NIV) ~ "'Show me, Lord, my life's end and the number of my days; let me know how fleeting my life is."

Me: "Lord, what do You want me to know today?"

God: "Surround yourself with people who will encourage you in your walk with Me. Let your conversation be pleasing in My sight, which means always. Remind yourself of My blessings daily so you will be less apt to complain. Meditate on My Word often. In this way, you will train yourself to conform to My image and will thus become a better reflection of Me in the sight of all who see you, even when you don't realize you're being watched."

1 Tim. 4:7-8 (NIV) ~ "Have nothing to do with godless myths and old wives' tales; rather, train yourself to be godly. For physical training is of some value, but godliness has value for all things, holding promise for both the present life and the life to come."

Me: "Lord, what do You want me to know today?"

God: "Prepare your heart for the transformation work I intend to accomplish in you; this will require much faith and complete obedience when I nudge you to submit to My will in areas where you've previously resisted My calling. Everything I have planned for you is for a good purpose, with eternal significance.

"Do not shrink back when I direct you to move forward. Cooperate with Me in every area, that your joy may be full. Then, you will know the extent of the fulfillment I created for you to experience in your lifetime."

Ps. 111:10 (NIV) ~ "The fear of the Lord is the beginning of wisdom; all who follow his precepts have good understanding. To him belongs eternal praise."

Me: "Lord, what do You want me to know today?"

God: "Apply to your everyday life those things I've been teaching you that need improvement in order that you may know more fully My will for you. When you make an effort to rid yourself of habits and thought patterns that create distance between you and Me, asking Me for help along the way, I will reveal to you what I want to fill those voids with in order that you may be rooted more firmly in My steadfast love for you, with your eyes ever fixed on Me.

"The closer you walk with Me, the more clearly you will see My perfect plans being fulfilled and understand how important your part in the whole picture is."

Col. 2:6-7 (NIV) ~ "So then, just as you received Christ Jesus as Lord, continue to live your lives in him, rooted and built up in him, strengthened in the faith as you were taught, and overflowing with thankfulness."

Me: "Lord, what do You want me to know today?"

God: "Certain things will always grasp for your attention. You know what these are in your life, and I know which of these things enhance your relationship with Me and which ones do not.

"When you stop and take a good look at how you spend your time, what do you see? Are you open to My leading in your day even if it conflicts with your own comfortable routine? Are you able to honestly say, 'Lord, here I am— use me as You desire today.'? Will you trust Me to steer you away from unhealthy habits, however painful the process, so that I can redirect your attention to the kingdom work I want you to complete in your lifetime?"

1 Pet. 5:8 (NIV) ~ "Be alert and of sober mind. Your enemy the devil prowls around like a roaring lion looking for someone to devour."

Me: "Lord, what do You want me to know today?"

God: "Like a beacon on a hill is the way My Word of Truth will shine into your life when you immerse yourself into reading it and becoming familiar with it so that you can apply it to your daily life situations. Do not skim over or ignore anything you come to in My Holy Word, but instead, ask Me how it applies to you and your relationship with Me, specifically. Listen for My answers to you, and follow My directions without wavering.

"The more you seek to know Me, the more My truth will be revealed to you. There is no end to what I will share with you when you seek Me above all else."

Ps. 119:2 (NIV) ~ "Blessed are those who keep his statutes and seek him with all their heart—"

Me: "Lord, what do You want me to know today?"

God: "Blessed are they who hear My Word and obey it. I will walk closely with them, leading and directing them in the way they should go. They will not be shaken when storms come, for I will be their strength and their shelter. They will lean on Me, and I will hold them up. They will never have reason to fear. Fear has lost its power at the cross of Calvary. 'It is finished.'"

Ps. 91:1 (NIV) ~ "Whoever dwells in the shelter of the Most High will rest in the shadow of the Almighty."

Me: "Lord, what do You want me to know today?"

God: "There will be times when you don't want to obey Me even though you do know what I'm asking of you. When you willingly obey Me anyway, there will be positive consequences in your own life and in the lives of others who may be directly affected by your choices. When you honor Me in this way, you will feel My Spirit of Peace living and working in you no matter what your current circumstances may be."

Ps. 119:134 (NIV) ~ "Redeem me from human oppression, that I may obey your precepts."

Me: "Lord, what do You want me to know today?"

God: "The size of the blessing does not correlate with the size of the assignment. Rather, the obedience of the heart directly affects the magnitude of the resulting blessings. When you act out of obedience to Me, you will see how I will multiply your offering of selfless service in ways you can't imagine."

Rom. 12:1 (NIV) ~ "Therefore, I urge you, brothers and sisters, in view of God's mercy, to offer your bodies as a living sacrifice, holy and pleasing to God—this is your true and proper worship."

Me: "Lord, what do You want me to know today?"

God: "Settle yourself in My presence, and allow My Spirit to direct your thoughts. Unless you purpose to listen intentionally, you will miss out on what I want to share with you. The same goes for your eyes—watch with purpose throughout your day for those miracles I've placed all around you, that you may see My glory even in the smallest circumstances.

"When I show you how I am at work in your life, don't hesitate to share this blessing with others; a thankful heart is contagious."

Is. 55:8-9 (NIV) ~ "'For my thoughts are not your thoughts, neither are your ways my ways,' declares the Lord. 'As the heavens are higher than the earth, so are my ways higher than your ways and my thoughts than your thoughts."

Me: "Lord, what do You want me to know today?"

God: "Distance yourself from any relationship, hobby, or other pursuit that threatens to take My place as first in your life. Do a thorough assessment of how you spend your time, and identify those things that encourage and inspire you in your walk with Me. Identify also those things that drain your energy with their constant demands on your time and attention, leaving you with little or no desire to spend time with Me. Then, ask Me to help you prioritize your hours and your days, and you will begin to understand what's purposeful in your life and what is not.

"I will teach you how to carve out time for Me, and you will see how everything else that's truly significant in your day, according to My perfect plan for you, will have its own allotted time for your enjoyment and fulfillment."

2 Sam. 22:30 (NIV) ~ "With your help I can advance against a troop; with my God I can scale a wall."

Me: "Lord, what do You want me to know today?"

God: "There will always be distractions in your day that will require you to refocus and readjust your expectations for how your time is spent. Some distractions are good—they give you opportunities to minister to others or rejoice with them, perhaps. When these things happen, do not grumble, but instead, thank Me for using you in a way that allows you to reflect My light of love within your area of influence.

"Always keep your eyes open to see the ways I am working in your life so you will not miss those faith-building moments that I send your way."

Ps. 7:17 (NIV) ~ "I will give thanks to the Lord because of his righteousness; I will sing the praises of the name of the Lord Most High."

Me: "Lord, what do You want me to know today?"

God: "Suppose there was a way that you could extract precious jewels from the dirt clods in your yard or garden. How much time would you spend with your hands in the dirt, intent on not overlooking a single opportunity to reap a valuable harvest?

"Now, imagine that those dirt clods represent the sin and darkness encasing the precious souls of your unsaved family and friends whom you love and treasure. Are you willing to get your hands dirty by coming alongside them in order that you may help them see how valuable they are to you and Me? They are priceless in My sight and so loved—they just can't see the light yet. Will you help them discover the truth of My love before it's too late?"

Gal. 6:9 (NIV) ~ "Let us not become weary in doing good, for at the proper time we will reap a harvest if we do not give up."

Me: "Lord, what do You want me to know today?"

God: "I have given you the means to accomplish all that I have instructed you to do so far. It's up to you to do your part now.

"Don't keep looking ahead all the time trying to figure out the next steps. Stay focused on the here and now, and celebrate even the smallest victories in your day. I will walk with you and direct your path; I have so much to show you along the way. Will you trust Me?"

Heb. 6:10-11 (NIV) ~ "God is not unjust; he will not forget your work and the love you have shown him as you have helped his people and continue to help them. We want each of you to show this same diligence to the very end, so that what you hope for may be fully realized."

Me: "Lord, what do You want me to know today?"

God: "Spend time in prayer every day. Look for pockets of time in your day where you can talk to Me on your own behalf and on behalf of others.

"Listen to the nudging of My Holy Spirit. When you sense a need to pray for someone, do not put it off till later. When I call My prayer warriors into action, the time is now. No matter how short your prayer may be, I will hear it and act upon it."

Col.1:9 (NIV) ~ "For this reason, since the day we heard about you, we have not stopped praying for you. We continually ask God to fill you with the knowledge of his will through all the wisdom and understanding that the Spirit gives,"

Me: "Lord, what do You want me to know today?"

God: "Resist the urge to be in control of situations that are Mine to handle. Allow Me to work out the best solution for every controversy that pops up and preoccupies your thoughts.

"You aren't meant to carry the heavy load that the burdens of a sinful world will heap upon your shoulders. Release it—give it all to Me through prayer and surrender. I will give you peace in return so that you may live life and live it abundantly as I designed for you to do."

Ps. 32:9-10 (NIV) ~ "Do not be like the horse or the mule, which have no understanding but must be controlled by bit and bridle or they will not come to you. Many are the woes of the wicked, but the Lord's unfailing love surrounds the one who trusts in him."

Made in the USA
Las Vegas, NV
29 August 2021